Ted,

[h]ope this book helps
[yo]ur understanding of
[th]e organizational & leadership
[d]ynamics that create the best of _____

Enjoy the read!

Bill

Praise for *Outfocus*

"A high impact read! Adams lays out a road map to shift from management to leadership by harnessing the power of collaboration. In a post-COVID world, the ability to build resilient, adaptive organizations—and leverage a performance platform for effective meeting management, robust decision-making, and impactful reporting—will determine success. Whether you are new to executive management or embarking on an innovative leadership venture, there is something here for everyone."

—*Shannon Lundquist*
Senior Partner and Federal Account Leader, Deloitte Canada

"Insightful and compelling, this book puts into perspective what it takes to effectively compete in the modern era. Adams succinctly captures the leadership challenge of the twenty-first century and then artfully explains how optimizing collaboration will maximize performance and move an organization closer toward excellence. A must-read for any executive who aspires to be a great leader. If this book doesn't motivate you to do everything possible to *OUTFOCUS* competitors, nothing will."

—*Vincent Zandvliet*
Former IBM Global Managing Director

"If you lead, then you should read *OUTFOCUS!* This book takes our understanding of leadership to a whole new level. Adams describes in vivid detail the challenges executives face managing in the never-fast-enough workplace of today. Coining the phrase "on-the-fly leadership" to represent how leaders lead, Adams presents a disruptive approach that redefines how we think, act, and work in team environments to drive results. To say this book is a game changer is an understatement; it's a mindset changer."

—*Barbara Miller*
Former VP Global Sourcing and Data Management,
AmerisourceBergen

"Simplify workplace complexity! This is the overarching message carried throughout the book. Regardless of industry or size of company, Adams puts forth a recipe for achieving better and more consistent results. Readers will find themselves rising above the endless noise and the mind-numbing minutiae as they turn the pages and learn how to lead teams with calculated and deliberate action. Enabling focus, alignment, accountability, and nimble decision-making, Bill's approach with his Performance Automation Platform is emblematic of the future of work."

—*Dan Taylor*
President, Guidacent Consulting

OUTFOCUS

BILL ADAMS JR.

HARNESS THE
POWER OF COLLABORATION

ForbesBooks

Published by ForbesBooks, Charleston, South Carolina.
Member of Advantage Media Group.

ForbesBooks is a registered trademark, and the ForbesBooks colophon is a trademark of Forbes Media, LLC.

10 9 8 7 6 5 4 3 2 1

ISBN: 978-1-95086-397-6
LCCN: 2021924778

This custom publication is intended to provide accurate information and the opinions of the author in regard to the subject matter covered. It is sold with the understanding that the publisher, Advantage|ForbesBooks, is not engaged in rendering legal, financial, or professional services of any kind. If legal advice or other expert assistance is required, the reader is advised to seek the services of a competent professional.

 Advantage Media Group is proud to be a part of the Tree Neutral® program. Tree Neutral offsets the number of trees consumed in the production and printing of this book by taking proactive steps such as planting trees in direct proportion to the number of trees used to print books. To learn more about Tree Neutral, please visit www.treeneutral.com.

Since 1917, Forbes has remained steadfast in its mission to serve as the defining voice of entrepreneurial capitalism. ForbesBooks, launched in 2016 through a partnership with Advantage Media Group, furthers that aim by helping business and thought leaders bring their stories, passion, and knowledge to the forefront in custom books. Opinions expressed by ForbesBooks authors are their own. To be considered for publication, please visit www.forbesbooks.com.

*This book is dedicated to my loving wife and business partner, Linda,
who has encouraged and supported me in all of life's endeavors,
including the writing of this book. Of all our business journeys, this one
may have been the most difficult of all—thank you, my love.*

CONTENTS

TARGA

Targa Targa is the first AI-driven SaaS Performance Automation Platform (PAP) that helps organizations harness the power of collaboration and gain a competitive advantage. Progressive leaders frustrated and disoriented by using fragmented resources to manage the day-to-day business process gravitate to this true performance game changer because it helps them keep a finger on the pulse of team progress anywhere, anytime.

Specifically designed to evolve the long-heralded hybrid workforce concept, the platform enables humans, robots, and systems to work synergistically in driving business results. Touted by many leading management authorities as the next generation step toward fully democratizing knowledge across the enterprise, it simplifies workplace complexity and lightens the workload on the workforce.

To accomplish this end, Targa, unlike any other performance collaboration platform, uniquely auto-syncs team activities, integrates third-party data, automates tasks, and augments decision-making—all on a single platform. And for the first time, leaders can manage performance on any device using Hubbi, the first performance command bot that empowers leaders to manage business operations hands-free through voice-activated technology.

To learn more about how Targa can help your organization, please visit our website at https://targatek.com/ or call Bill directly at 973-714-9228.

CONSULT WHITESPACE LLC

A management consulting and market research firm specializing in business model renewal and organizational transformation since 1998, Whitespace has amassed an outstanding record of success. The firm's focus was initially helping leadership teams from the C-suite to line managers in *Fortune* 50 and high-growth companies resolve a wide variety of business performance challenges.

With that experience in hand, the firm's founder and the author of this book—Bill Adams—today acts as a strategic thought leader facilitating change and transformation efforts, coaching leadership teams on how to think, act, and work as one in the process of producing results. He is a confidant to leaders looking to strengthen their core leadership skills and expand their sphere of influence over the workforce to get a leg up on being a great leader.

Acting as a facilitator, coach, and advisor, Adams leverages the concepts, methodologies, and tools found throughout the pages of this book. Working solo or with a small team of support professionals, Adams carefully selects assignments that can truly use his expertise to move an organization forward and whose leaders are open and willing to embrace his forward-thinking notion that there exists a deep-seated link between collaboration, performance, and excellence.

To learn more about Bill's services, please visit our website at http://www.whitespacellc.com/ or call Bill directly at 973-714-9228.

ACKNOWLEDGMENTS

No author can write a book without the cooperation of many individuals, and *OUTFOCUS* is no exception. I begin by thanking the many consultants, business associates, and academics that I had the great pleasure to work with over my career who in some way contributed to the concepts, models, and tools that are contained in these pages.

A special thanks goes to Jim Champy, organizational theorist and coauthor of the *New York Times* best seller *Reengineering the Corporation.* As chairman of consulting at Dell/Perot Systems, I had the great pleasure of working alongside Jim after Perot Systems acquired my management consulting firm, Infosource. Acting in the capacity of strategic alliance advisor and contributing to his book *X-Engineering the Corporation* triggered the underlying theories that support my approach to innovation and transformation called Outcome Dynamics. Jim is a mentor and a friend. He helped me evolve the underlying concepts and steadfastly reinforced the use of its application in the field. Many thanks, my friend; you remain a special person in my life.

A great debt of gratitude goes to Richard Chamberlain, a longtime colleague and friend. Certified in Outcome Dynamics, he encouraged the writing of this book long before a word was penned.

When we met, Richard was a VP at Fujitsu Consulting. Instantly, we found common ground discussing the paradigm shift occurring in organizational life. As a performance and quality expert with a Sixth Sigma Black Belt, he gravitated to my theory that the secret to maximizing performance lies in the ability of companies to optimize collaboration. Burning the midnight oil, he helped me turned theory into reality. He remains a personal advisor to me, providing valuable insight on performance challenges that face leaders today. Thank you, my friend. The journey was long but memorable.

My sincere appreciation goes out to Vik Kasturi, founder and president of Digitivity. As our firm's interim chief technology officer, his experience contributed valuable insight to the writing of this book. As a strategic technology consultant to *Fortune* 100 companies and lead consultant on positioning Google G-Suite and Microsoft Azure in the market, his perspective on the role that technology plays in organization life was indispensable. His guidance on how technology is changing the face of work is woven throughout the pages of this book. He helped me understand the many ways that advanced technology influences the future of work. His depth and breadth of knowledge regarding how AI-enabled automation is reshaping the very nature of work is captivating. You have taught me much, sir, and I deeply appreciate it.

A loud shout-out goes to my daughter, Natalie Metchnik, VP of onboarding and implementation in our firm. Her insights and ideas from a millennial perspective were instrumental in forging our understanding of where future leaders are headed. I found her keen sensibilities and intuition as to what matters most with young leaders to be not only on point, but inspiring. Her insights on the workplace of the future are dotted throughout this book. Thank you, my dear. I could not be prouder.

A special recognition goes out to the team at Advantage|ForbesBooks. Without their belief that the subject matter contained in this book is noteworthy and relevant to modern-day leadership, it would not have come to market with such fervor. Their passion and insight to prepare the book for market acceptance was invaluable. Going through their extensive vetting process and having the book associated with their brand was an investment well worth making. They brought the book to life by rounding out the edges and making it a more enjoyable experience for the reader. I would highly recommend their approach to any author who seeks to be a thought leader in their area of expertise.

Many thanks to the organizations that added insight throughout the book (e.g., Amazon, Google, Automation Anywhere, McKinsey, Gartner, Deloitte, PwC, Forrester Research, IDC Research). Their research studies and experience helped support many of the ideas and theories found throughout the book. And many thanks to the experts and business leaders who agreed to be interviewed in the last chapter of this book. Their perspective on my assertion that addressing the convergence of technology and the human element is the challenge of the twenty-first century added richness to the book, helping readers to form their own opinions.

I have espoused the philosophy that, in the end, the only things that really matter in life are your family, friends, and the memories that they produce. In writing this book, I had the great pleasure of working with a few family members and many friends, which produced lasting memories that, in the words of an old but memorable Mastercard commercial, are priceless!

FOREWORD

Bill Adams's eye-opening book takes you on a mesmerizing journey into the complex world of collaboration, where technology and the human element battle in what he calls the "convergence challenge." How leaders contend with the convergence is the leadership challenge of the twenty-first century, especially in the aftermath of the pandemic.

As a physician and chairman and CEO of a NASDAQ healthcare company, I had the unique opportunity to see the devastation that COVID-19 caused while acting as an advisor to governors in the northeastern part of the United States. Fortuitously, there are many lessons to learn from the pandemic about life, and there is no lesson more consequential than the realization that nothing is sacrosanct to change, including organizational life.

As an investor and board member in several technology companies, it never ceases to amaze me how quickly technology is changing every aspect of organizational life. Even the way in which we think about and manage business is perpetual, and we are always searching for better tools to promote collaboration.

This book has made me even more aware of the link between collaboration and performance. To be blunt, the way we executives run ourselves ragged trying to manage organizational performance using today's disconnected tools leaves much to be desired. The author's ability to communicate the challenges and opportunities that lie ahead in this regard is nothing short of stupefying.

> To be blunt, the way we executives run ourselves ragged trying to manage organizational performance using today's disconnected tools leaves much to be desired.

I applaud Adams for recognizing the underlying conditions occurring in organizational life that affect every dimension of leadership. His grasp on where the workplace is headed and the role that collaboration plays in its future is not only insightful, but consequential. His ability to sense the intangible forces that push against executives as they struggle to manage the business is perspicacious.

Bill's inference that, to be successful, leaders must leverage the hybrid workforce concept and automate as much low-value work as possible is unavoidable. He clearly articulates throughout the book why there may be no more important aspect to leadership than knowing how to select the right technology and make the right organization moves to optimize collaboration.

That's why this book is so welcome. In *OUTFOCUS*, Adams lays out a compelling case for why optimizing the collaborative process improves performance and enables executives to see what competitors can't. He expounds on the many ways that a modern-day condition he calls on-the-fly leadership impacts Core Leadership Functions and the ability to focus their attention, both of which I experience everyday leading my firm.

It is welcome because Adams has done the hard work of distilling the underlying dynamics of organization life and what constitutes good leadership in the twenty-first century. His conclusion that there is a direct link between collaboration and performance that moves an organization toward excellence is undeniable.

I have firsthand knowledge of how Bill's consulting approach, Outcome Dynamics, works. Sitting on the board of Datatec, a NASDAQ technology company, we developed a project management software product. The executive team and the board were in a quandary as to what the best course of action would be to optimize its value. Bill led several sessions with the board and executive team until it became evident that an IPO was the best course of action.

The board, being sufficiently impressed, offered Adams a board seat, which he accepted. As our business strategist, he led the IPO initiative with Bear Sterns. I was personally impressed with him to the point that I became a special healthcare advisor in his consulting firm, Whitespace. I watched Adams, as a strategic thought leader, help executives move their business model forward and transform organizational dynamics to support them.

Adams is a true thought leader. He glibly claims: "Innovation is not only my life's work; it's part of my DNA." He gets how organization and leadership work in both theory and practice. As you turn the pages of this book, listen carefully to what he has to say. If it doesn't motivate you to do everything in your power to build the collaborative organization of tomorrow, nothing will!

—*Dr. David Milch*
Chairman, Healthcare Capital Corp.

MUST READ FIRST!

Welcome to the great transition, a spectacle that eclipses the Industrial Revolution. As we wave goodbye to the information age and say hello to the collaboration age, a seismic paradigm shift is occurring in organizational life. With this new age, democratizing knowledge is the crucible to succeed, and collaboration is the vehicle to get the job done.

Over the past decade, every aspect of organization life has been turned upside down. The workplace has become an ever-more chaotic and complex environment to manage organizational performance. Workloads have hit all-time highs, and leaders continue to struggle with the weight of decision-making and reporting responsibilities.

Juggling a multitude of fragmented resources and business intelligence (BI) tools to manage operations has proved to be woefully inadequate. Leaders find that their productivity greatly suffers using a hodgepodge of resources, and they are consistently frustrated with their inability to keep a finger on the pulse of team performance. To make matters worse, wading through the mountain of data they produce to manage performance often disorients them. Truly, business leadership today ain't what it used to be!

The need for leaders to out-collaborate competitors is fierce, and every company is competing in the race whether they acknowledge it or not. According to Advantage|ForbesBooks Vice President Alison Morse, a seasoned veteran of the publishing business, "The hottest nonfiction topic and best-selling books relate to collaboration. Executives have an extraordinary appetite for the subject, especially since the pandemic."

> Leaders find that their productivity greatly suffers using a hodgepodge of resources, and they are consistently frustrated with their inability to keep a finger on the pulse of team performance.

Focusing on collaboration in the age of collaboration certainly makes sense. But it's not that simple. At the epicenter of the convergence is a tug-of-war between the pull of technology and the pull of human resistance. Critical to addressing the convergence is understanding the dynamics that surround it and how collaboration plays a central role in it.

We live in an age where "instantaneous equates to competitiveness," to quote the renowned Harvard Business School professor Michael Porter. Leaders find themselves almost breathless at the end of the day, flying between meetings trying to capture, analyze, and share information using a menagerie of fragmented resources and BI tools.

Many leaders have come to the shocking conclusion that never catching up is the new normal. One senior leader told me that acceptance of the situation was key to maintain his sanity. Another leader told me that regardless of how many hours she puts in, she never gets caught up, so why bother? These are sure signs that the great transition is taking its toll on leaders as poor organizational performance continues to rip apart the bottom line of companies.

Research studies from some of the most predominant firms (e.g., McKinsey, Deloitte, and PwC) conclude that losses due to poor performance have dramatically increased over the past decade, and this trend continues to rise. *Fortune* 500 companies alone from 2016 to 2019 lost on average $20 billion to $30 billion annually. These are staggering numbers given all the advances made in technology to help leaders manage operations.

Imagine that just a 10 percent improvement in performance adds an aggregate of $2 billion to $3 billion to the bottom line of *Fortune* 500 companies alone. This is found money! And there is no better way to get there than to focus on improving the collaborative process, as this book will explain.

As the paradigm shift continues to shake organizational life to its foundation, leaders are bombarded with the latest and greatest collaboration tools to help them keep pace. But do not be fooled—adding more of the same tools in the toolbox is not the answer. Our research found that additional tools will only further complicate and do not simplify workplace dynamics. From a collaboration perspective, the tools we use today just don't work well!

They don't work well because they open the door for disconnects, bottlenecks, and voids to creep into the collaborative process. These are the true villains of collaboration, as they gum up the works. They are the reason that leaders feel frustrated and disoriented. And they are the primary reason that poor performance continues to rise.

In the wake of the transition, we identified a modern-day phenomenon that I dubbed "on-the-fly leadership." The term depicts exactly how leaders lead in the never-fast-enough workplace of today. Leaders no longer have the luxury of pondering decisions for days or even hours. They must be able to make sound decisions on-the-fly, which means they must have the right information in the right form at the right time.

The problem is that much of the information today is not available when it is most needed or in the form that is most useful. Too often it comes packaged in time-bound reports that capture pieces of the total picture. Disjointed, stale information is not a healthy situation for on-the-fly decision makers.

The inability of leaders to know where teams stand in producing results at any given time speaks volumes about the lackluster way in which we collaborate today. Leaders no longer have time to arm wrestle information out of teams during meetings, and they can ill afford the daisy chain of emails, voice mails, and text messages after a meeting to get the information. Passing the baton of information between coworkers and leaders can no longer be a human-bound task, as this book shall illuminate.

The fallout of on-the-fly leadership is evident everywhere. In chapter one, you'll learn how the fallout impacts the Core Leadership Functions: meeting management, decision-making, and reporting. These functions consume the majority of leaders' time and have the greatest impact on organizational performance.

Studies have shown that on average 70 to 75 percent of a leader's time is somehow involved with these three leadership functions. Our research corroborates these statistics. We further deduced that the mastery that leaders have over these functions greatly influences the overall performance of the organization. The fruits of this research are contained in the pages of this book.

Our research also found that leading on-the-fly creates a blowback effect on the ability of leaders to focus on the things that matter when they matter. I refer to this egregious condition as Attention Deficit Syndrome. You will learn how the syndrome manifests itself and how to counter its effects in chapter two. Like any syndrome, it comes with a host of unwanted symptoms that no leader, great or otherwise, can escape—bar none!

In chapter three, you will learn the organizational aspects of the convergence. It explains why moving the organization toward open-border structures encourages the worker participation necessary to optimize the collaborative process and why work systems that support the business structures must be flexible and scalable to quickly react to fluid market and competitor conditions.

This book is an outgrowth of my firm's twenty-five years of research and management consulting experience. Experts in innovation and transformation, the firm has leveraged its proprietary approach—Outcome Dynamics—to help resolve business performance challenges within client organizations. Working closely with leadership teams from the C-suite to line managers in *Fortune* 50 to high-growth companies, we witnessed firsthand the impact that the paradigm shift is having on organizational life and, by extension, the rules for good leadership.

The book draws upon the results of these studies and that of selected studies conducted by high-profile research firms, academics, and consultants. The studies we conducted for clients are called Value Dynamics Testing. The results of these studies were aggregated under an umbrella study titled "Organization and Market Dynamics."

The objective of these studies was to determine how client business models fared against market and competitive conditions and then to determine how modifications to the model would help to out-position competitors or potentially disrupt a market altogether. Over the years, we learned a lot about the changes occurring in organizational dynamics through these studies.

Concurrently, our firm conducted an in-house study titled "What Makes Leaders Tick." It identified the critical factors that separate good from great leaders, pinpointing the qualities and skills necessary to remain on the forefront of good leadership. The results of these studies are reflected throughout this book.

Through our research and consulting experience, we recognized that the convergence of technology and the human element was a looming problem. We further recognized that leaders need to contend with the convergence challenge today if they want to remain competitive tomorrow.

In our effort to understand the underlying dynamics involved in the challenge, we discovered that there exists a profound link between collaboration and performance—improve the former and the latter will follow. This eyebrow-raiser placed the importance of collaboration in the crosshairs of our endeavor to help leaders lead.

> Leaders need to contend with the convergence challenge today if they want to remain competitive tomorrow.

In chapter four, you will learn why leveraging advanced technology to optimize collaboration is tantamount to good leadership and why leaders who take full advantage of advanced technologies in building the collaborative organization of tomorrow will be handsomely rewarded while unparticipating leaders will have to face the competitive consequences.

Although advances in technology over the last decade have been significant, they are not always being optimized. Chapter four will examine why leaders are not receiving the full benefits that technology has to offer because of this. It will also highlight why organizations that continue to promulgate a "get-by" mentality toward technology are competitively vulnerable. Clearly, leaders stand at a crossroads!

Over the years, I have spent considerable time thinking and writing about the convergence of technology and the human element. This area of study naturally relates to and augments my work on organization and leadership. One thing is clear: leadership today is exactly what it was during the Industrial Revolution—influencing people to action. The technology may be dramatically different, but the resolve of progressive leaders needed to influence the workforce to action remains intact.

In the fifth chapter, you will be exposed to Targa—an AI-driven Performance Automation Platform (PAP) that enables organizations to attain hyper-collaboration, be it for a team, department, division, or across the entire enterprise. As part of a three-pronged approach to collaborating, the platform redefines what it means to collaborate in the age of collaboration.

To further help leaders negotiate the convergence challenge, I created the Five Focus Factors. One factor at a time is presented at the end of the first five chapters. Each factor is supported by three salient points taken from the chapter. Together, they are a road map to help leaders build the collaborative organization of tomorrow.

Chapter six pulls it all together. Performance experts and senior operating executives from various industries weigh in with their opinion on the convergence challenge. They provide insight into the dynamics that surround the challenge, explaining why this is the time to capitalize on the convergence. This chapter is intended to provide a well-rounded view of the challenge from different vantage points so that readers can form a more rational opinion about the matters at hand.

When confronted with any significant change, the first and primary issues are openness and willingness. To successfully transform into a truly collaborative organization, everyone involved must be open and willing to examine attitudes and modify behaviors. Failure to do so can end in disaster.

Experts from economists to social scientists concur that although the great transition is in full swing, it's still in its infancy. They also claim that the greatest impact will be felt by the burgeoning sector of the workforce referred to as information workers (IWs). They are the backbone of the modern organization and therefore the focus of this book.

IW activities are diverse and far-reaching. They are the caregivers of the critical information necessary to produce results. If leaders are to be successful at the convergence, then IWs must understand the need for it and buy into it. This is a true test of leadership.

In the decades ahead, we will see unprecedented, breathtaking changes that will take collaboration to new heights. Information will flow freely—almost effortlessly—to those who need it, when they need it. This is the hallmark of the collaborative organization that every leader should aspire to while contending with the convergence challenge.

The train is leaving the station. No leader should be left behind. My question to you is, are you willing to get on board? Are you willing to take on the convergence challenge and forge the collaborative organization of tomorrow? Perhaps more importantly, are you cognizant of the competitive ramifications if you do not participate?

Leaders stand at the crossroads. If the path you choose is to move forward, then I invite you to continue reading. This book will take you on an unimaginable journey, showing you how to harness the power of collaboration to *outfocus* competitors and gain the competitive advantage.

Footnote: Throughout the book, everyone from the C-suite to line managers is considered a leader. At the beginning of each chapter, there is a section titled "What and Why of Focus." It reveals what the focus of the chapter is on and identifies two of the most important obstacles that must be addressed to succeed as a leader. At the end of each chapter, there is a section titled "Focus Factor." Each factor is comprised of salient points taken from the chapter. When combined, they are a road map to help leaders build the collaborative organization of tomorrow.

COMPETITIVE ADVANTAGE

CHAPTER 1

ON-THE-FLY LEADERSHIP

What and Why of Focus

There is vast difference between leading and managing. The former is about commanding the workplace and influencing the workforce; the latter is more about administrating. Both are good and necessary. Great leaders want to know *what* to focus on to overcome the fallout that leading on-the-fly has on the Core Leadership Functions. These same leaders want to know *why* obstacles like contending with the "wave of resistance" and the relentless pressure to produce must not stand in the way.

DO MORE WITH LESS! This is the aim of the modern organization. The pressure on leaders to produce results quickly and accurately is inexorable. Many leaders have reached their capacity to cope and have simply acquiesced to the idea that they will never catch up. This is the plight of leadership today.

In this first chapter, we closely examine a modern-day phenomenon that I dubbed "on-the-fly leadership." The term aptly depicts how leaders lead in the never-fast-enough workplace of today. They fly from meeting to meeting, attempting to manage the business process with fragmented resources. This practice has brought organizational performance to its knees—crushing the bottom line!

Leaders no longer have the luxury of pondering decisions. They must be able to make sound decisions spontaneously, which requires them to have the right information at the right time and possess the right skills to convert that information into actionable solutions.

There is an exhausting number of resources (tools) available to help leaders manage workflow and operations. This makes one wonder why the gap between planning and execution continues to widen and poor performance continues to rise. The mishmash of resources to collaborate today just doesn't work well!

This situation is compounded by leaders using traditional time-bound reports that contain disjointed, stale information. These reports have leaders disoriented as to where teams stand at any given time. Leaders eventually believe they have lost control over the direction of team performance and feel vulnerable to failure.

After years of research and consulting to leadership teams, we realize that leaders are more frustrated and disoriented in managing the day-to-day business process than ever before. We further recognize that this occurrence is pervasive among leaders regardless of industry or size of company from the C-suite to line managers—and it's getting worse.

With data in hand, there is no doubt that this is not a passing fad but a current-day leadership phenomenon that comes with the transition between ages. To depict this phenomenon, I coined the term "on-the-fly leadership." Leading on-the-fly has many dimensions that are changing the rules for good leadership.

I first recognized the phenomenon while auditing how leaders preside over meetings as part of Outcome Dynamics. Meetings are the first and most critical step in the process of democratizing knowledge, the crucible to success in the modern age. How well leaders and teams collaborate in meetings is a leading indicator of how they perform as an organization.

In 2016, I authored a white paper titled "On-the-Fly Leadership: Managing by Sound Bites, Metric Mania, and Egg Timers." It explained in detail what the phenomenon entails and how it impacts meeting dynamics and their outcome, adding that workplace complexity and work overload are driven by the proliferation of technology as the primary offenders. And it called out three unsavory pitfalls that cause meetings to be unproductive and, in some cases, counterproductive.

After more research and field experience around the on-the-fly phenomenon, I updated the white paper in 2018. It reaffirmed the conclusions arrived at in the initial white paper. However, it went on to explain how leading on-the-fly impacts the three most critical leadership functions: meeting management, decision-making, and reporting.

Referred to these elements as the Core Leader Functions, the paper presented third-party evidence that stated that, on average, 70 to 75 percent of a leader's time is spent performing these functions. It went on to explain that how leaders perform these functions directly affects the overall performance of the organization. Mundane as they may seem on the surface, they are the make-or-break functions that separate good from great leaders, as this chapter will highlight.

In addition, the paper expounded on why workplace complexity and work overload act like a "wave of resistance" pushing against all efforts on the part of leaders to move the organization forward. The presence of this invisible force is indisputable and formidable. The paper discussed why leaders must learn to contend with these rogue forces if they are to succeed.

The paper finally explained why using the fragmented resources to manage the day-to-day business process just doesn't work well and how the unfettered growth of BI tools further disorients leaders, adding to their frustration.

Look around you. Our lives are consumed with snapshots. This trend goes far beyond organizational life, touching every aspect of our daily activities. Information is condensed into bite-size nuggets so more can be consumed in less time, and there is no turning back as advances in technology continue to promulgate the trend.

Tools like Twitter and Snapchat are the communication mode of choice for young leaders, replacing an older generation of leaders who rely on Facebook for their communication. Going forward, experts in many disciplines are convinced that technology advances will find their way into organizational life far more quickly than they have in the past.

Besides taking advantage of technology, leading on-the-fly requires adopting a "no-detail" mentality. Leaders are forced to do this if they want to keep pace in the never-fast-enough workplace of today. Constantly under the gun to make decisions on-the-fly, leaders cannot afford to get caught up in the weeds of details, and yet they must have sufficient information to make informed decisions.

> Besides taking advantage of technology, leading on-the-fly requires adopting a "no-detail" mentality. Leaders are forced to do this if they want to keep pace in the never-fast-enough workplace of today.

Our firm faced the same challenge. Over time, we have developed several "snapshot" tools to help resolve business performance challenges in client organizations. As an example, we have a snapshot tool to quickly assess the capacity and capability of leaders to perform. Dividing leadership into three qualities, traits, skills, and knowledge, I can quickly get a read on the strengths and weaknesses of leaders.

I refer to this snapshot tool as Qualities Assessment. With it, I can quickly ascertain much about an individual, whether it be in business, sports, or other life pursuits. Each quality is defined below.

1. **Traits**—attitude, aspiration, heart. *Desire to perform.*

2. **Skills**—competency, capability, aptitude. *Talent to perform.*

3. **Knowledge**—understanding, comprehension, mastery. *Grasp to perform.*

A second example of a snapshot tool is used to determine how leaders perform the Core Leadership Functions. Repeatedly, I find that there is a direct correlation between the proficiency of leaders to perform the core functions and the performance of their organization. Deemed as the Function Assessment Tool, it is a mechanism to quickly discern patterns of strengths and weaknesses in leaders.

Certainly, there is more to understanding the value of employees than by simply performing a Qualities and Function Assessment. Notwithstanding the fact that HR departments assess a multitude of aspects to gauge the value of an employee, if leaders can achieve an 80 percent accuracy rate in assessing individual qualities, then it may be worth adding these snapshot tools to your leadership tool kit.

Throughout these pages, several more snapshot tools will be introduced. Keep in mind that although our firm has used them in our consulting practice to help clients resolve business performance challenges, leaders can use them independently to do the same in their organizations.

Learning how to lead with a no-detail mentality is tricky but important. Recognizing this as a fact of modern organizational life is the first step to improving leadership skills, and those who do this well will have a leg up on becoming a great leader.

Before starting our journey together, let's put our first stake in the ground. Tom Peters, the leading authority on excellence and the author of several books on the subject, constantly reminds us: "We are in an age of unimaginable change and every leader should be keenly aware of where they stand in the race to gain the competitive advantage through collaboration."

Peters articulates the case made in this book perfectly. Only through collaboration can an organization gain the competitive advantage. When leaders contend with the convergence of technology and the human element, they must focus on optimizing the collaborative process. But contending with the convergence is no simple task.

Imagine it as a tug-of-war between the pull of technology and the pull of human resistance. Gartner, the leading technology research firm on the planet, claims it to be one of the most important challenges leaders face today. The need for leaders to contend with the convergence transcends industry and company size. With this said, leaders from all walks should take notice, as there is much at stake if you do not know how to *outfocus* competitors to gain the advantage.

Before moving on, let's place another stake in the ground concerning excellence. Much has been written on the subject, and many academic institutions, consultants, and coaches help leaders understand the various aspects of excellence. Over the last decade, building high-performance teams to achieve excellence has been the rage. I have consulted with a few companies whose sole purpose was to win the coveted Baldridge Award for their industry. This is a destination approach to excellence.

For our purpose, we again look to Tom Peters. He views excellence as "a never-ending pursuit—not a destination," and I could not agree more. Given the volatile market and competitive conditions that exist today, it is very sage advice. We embrace this approach as "true north" throughout the book, where excellence is seen as a moving target to be chased, not to be caught.

Progressive leaders get this. They continually strive to take their game to the next level, realizing that excellence today will not be excellence tomorrow. Winning the race to gain the competitive advantage makes perfect sense to them, especially in the post-COVID world where collaboration has been kicked into overdrive.

One last word. Planning, especially strategic planning, is not part of the core functions for a good reason. Leaders do not spend that much time on strategic planning. Estimates from management and leadership experts show that leaders dedicate 10 to 15 percent of their time to strategic matters (unless one happens to be in the strategic planning department of a large company).

Moreover, execution instead of planning is the cause of poor organizational performance, and it's more critical to address the space between the two than focusing on one or the other. Therefore the focus of this book is the space between planning and execution.

Leaders struggle to keep pace and find it difficult, if not impossible, to focus on strategic matters. As the book will explain, strategic planning is an extremely important part of good leadership, but the multitude of tactical matters that persistently tug at the sleeves of leaders leave little time to focus on it.

Case in Point: President—Business Strategy Consulting Firm

This highbrow strategy technology consulting firm headquartered in Seattle, Washington, boasts a stellar client list that includes Starbucks, FOSS, Costco, Nordstrom, and Microsoft.

In an interview with the president regarding planning, he shared:

Building out a business plan once a year and then reviewing that plan quarterly (or sometimes even just at performance review time) puts an organization at great risk of being on the losing end of any competitive race. Strategies and initiatives need to be reviewed routinely, fine-tuned, and often reprioritized or replaced by more relevant programs and tactics to stay ahead and accomplish business objectives.

This president believes that executives are missing the point trying to manage the modern-day organization using old-school planning techniques. He thinks that achieving excellence requires planning to be an integral part of the collaborative process from goal setting through execution.

He further commented:

> The proliferation of collaboration tools and knee-jerk reactions by companies to continually seek to implement the latest instant communication, file sharing, and alert systems often creates confusion and sensory overload in the work environment. And none of these so-called collaboration tools promote the necessary accountability or timely decision-making to stay aligned with goals and activities to get things done efficiently and build executive teamwork.

This president's articulation of the challenge to close the widening gap between planning and execution is extraordinary. His multi-decade tenure as an executive at American Express and now president of a strategy consulting firm has placed him on both sides of the desk—so if anyone would know the importance of collaboration in planning, he would.

Core Leadership Functions

Far and away, the functions of meeting management, decision-making, and reporting consume leaders' time. They are the key functions when it comes to improving the space between planning and execution. In fact, good leadership depends on how well leaders perform these functions because mastery over them is the only way to improve the performance of an organization.

The remainder of this chapter is dedicated to understanding how the fallout of on-the-fly leadership impacts the ability of leaders to perform the Core Leadership Functions. It explains in detail why the interdependence of the three functions maximizes performance and moves the organization closer toward excellence, the "holy grail" of performance.

MEETING MANAGEMENT

In organizational life, it is impossible to achieve both individual and organizational goals without the effective use of communication channels. Although there are many different techniques of communication, there is a consensus among performance experts that the most effective organizational communication occurs during meetings.

Over my consulting career, I have worked with leaders who believed that improving meeting management skills was trite and, in some cases, a waste of time. And, as you could guess, many of these leaders were the worst offenders. Look at it this way: proficiently conducting meetings is the linchpin to democratizing knowledge and is therefore a critical part of good leadership.

In our study "What Makes Leaders Tick," we found that leaders either promote or hinder team dynamics, which in turn has a direct impact on meeting outcomes. Meetings are central to create and transfer information to coworkers and leaders. They are the lifeblood of the organization, without which there would be no results. So take them seriously!

Presiding over meetings is not only a vital part of leadership; statistically, it is the greatest time consumer of the three Core Leadership Functions. In a significant study published in the *Journal of Business Research* in 2017, employees from forty-one countries provided comments on the effectiveness of their typical meetings and how to improve effectiveness.

Less than half of the respondents described meetings as an effective use of time. More recent studies have gone further, suggesting that many meetings are counterproductive. Since virtual meetings have ballooned, it's scary to consider what the results would tell us today. Running productive meetings may just be the Achilles' heel of leadership.

There are many resources to help leaders improve how they conduct meetings (e.g., books, videos, educational material, coaching, and consulting). However, even with all the help available, this critical function has proven to be an underdeveloped, underappreciated aspect of leadership. Proof of this can be seen everywhere as authorities across many disciplines claim that poor meetings remain a significant drag on organizational performance.

To support this statement, I cite a 2020 *Harvard Business Review* article on meetings titled "Stop the Meeting Madness." In it, they conclude that

> meetings have increased in length and frequency over the past fifty years to the point where executives spend an average of nearly twenty-three hours a week in them, up from less than ten hours per week in the sixties. And that doesn't even include all the impromptu gatherings that don't make it onto the schedule.

To quantify the impact of poor meetings on bottom-line performance, a Doodle's study titled "State of Meetings Report" published in 2020 concluded, "The cost of poorly organized meetings in 2019 reached $399 billion in the US and $58 billion in the UK. Combined, that is almost half a trillion dollars. This is a tremendous drag on performance and the effectiveness of business."

These studies leave little doubt that "meeting madness" is a real phenomenon and they have a significant impact on bottom-line performance when poorly run. More shocking is that the problem is getting worse, not better, especially as the burgeoning IWs grapple with distantly managing the business process.

In the post-COVID world, leaders find themselves flying between virtual sessions using communication tools like Zoom, WebEx, GoTo-Meeting, or Chime. But do not be fooled. These tools are meant to achieve face time between parties but do not help leaders to manage the business process one iota. Leaders find using these tools to run meetings adds to workplace complexity and work overload, placing more pressure on them to keep pace.

As the *Harvard Business Review* article and Doodle's findings confirm, when leaders conduct meetings poorly, it impacts team dynamics in the micro view and costs companies real money in the macro view. Below are three meeting pitfalls that are a fallout of on-the-fly leadership with a brief description of each.

> When leaders conduct meetings poorly, it impacts team dynamics in the micro view and costs companies real money in the macro view.

Sound Bite Management

The first disturbing pitfall is how leaders gather information in meetings to formulate decisions with a no-detail mentality. The distilling of information is required to keep pace; that is a fact of organizational life. Condensing complex information down to a few words or data points can be tricky. Finding the right balance between too much information and not enough to make good decisions is of primary concern.

I refer to this pitfall as Sound Bite Management. This Morse code-like mechanism to condense information into bite-size nuggets can be problematic if not performed properly. Leaders must avoid this pitfall or find themselves in an endless game of tag doing follow-ups. This is the real time waster.

Developing meeting management skills is anything but a waste of time. There are many far-reaching benefits to getting it right. This is low-hanging fruit for leaders to improve meeting outcomes.

Metric Mania

The next disturbing pitfall is how leaders look to metrics as the end-all and be-all to manage meetings. Of course, gauging and supporting decisions using key performance indicators (KPIs) or objectives and key results (OKRs) is a crucial dimension of leadership. However, too much of a good thing can be a bad thing. Overdependence on metrics when running meetings can be problematic to their outcome.

Metrics are a vital part of running meetings. However, to view them as the centerpiece around which meetings are conducted is sheer folly. McKinsey, in a 2018 article regarding meetings, states, "The number of metrics available today far exceeds the capability of managers to fully utilize them."

The message is clear: be mindful of the quality and quantity of metrics used to run meetings. To borrow a cliché, leaders who over-rely on metrics can end up with paralysis through analysis, which can deteriorate team dynamics and lead to poor meeting outcomes.

I refer to this pitfall as Metric Mania Management. Leaders will continue to be inundated with new ways to slice and dice data. However, be aware of those metrics that you consider "core" and those that can be considered "fringe." Metrics, for the most part, keep score of where teams stand to goal.

The question is not whether metrics are important—they are. It's more about deciding which ones to focus on in meetings to improve the quality of the outcomes. Nothing can impact team dynamics and meeting outcomes more than leaders who show signs of paralysis through analysis.

Egg Timer Management

The final pitfall deals with the amount of time leaders have in meeting to gather, analyze, and share information. Flying between meetings to keep initiatives and action items on track to achieve goals can be overwhelming.

Leaders today conduct and attend over 50 percent more meetings than just ten years ago. Korn Ferry, a leading consulting and executive recruiting firm, claims, "The amount of time leaders spend in a meeting on any one aspect of an issue is about six to eight minutes."

This is the time it takes to boil an egg and is the eight-hundred-pound gorilla, or should I say egg, sitting in the room that can affect team dynamics and cause poor outcomes.

Leaders walk the tightrope of time every day. They spend more time preparing and conducting meetings than anything else. It is the first and perhaps the most important step in the process of democratizing knowledge.

I refer to this pitfall as Egg Timer Management. Leaders must be cognizant that while capturing information in meetings, they have on average between six and eight minutes to focus on any one aspect of a topic. Thus, time spent in meetings must be carefully doled out to ensure that topics on the agenda are covered, but not to the point of infringing on team dynamics.

The pitfalls of leading by sound bites, metric mania, and egg timers are prevalent in today's on-the-fly workplace. Regardless of their state in organizational life, leaders must contend with these pitfalls when running meetings. Each pitfall on its own can have a negative impact on meeting outcomes. Altogether, they can devastate meeting outcomes.

The reality is that leaders go into meetings knowing things are behind schedule and that things may not be properly attended to.

Statistically, the number one reason for meetings in the first place is to uncover where teams stand on goals and to steer a course of corrective action, making them tactical in nature.

The amount of research conducted annually on meeting management is significant. Every year, researchers end up scratching their heads, wondering why the quality of meetings are getting worse, not better. This paradox is mind-blowing when considering the amount of technology available to make meetings more productive.

METHOD FOR MEETINGS

Now that we have briefly discussed the meeting pitfalls, let's turn our attention to the methods used to run meetings. By most accounts, there are four activities that dominate meeting dynamics. These activities account for almost 90 percent of the time spent in meetings, according to meeting management experts and my observations. Below, each activity is identified and defined.

- **Debriefing**—where do we stand?

- **Corrective Action**—what needs to be done?

- **Assigning action item**—who is going to do what?

- **Strategizing**—where do we go from here?

On average, the amount of time spent performing each function corresponds to the order listed. For example, meeting experts say that the activity of debriefing could take up to 40 percent of meeting time. This fact probably stuns no leader. The act of debriefing means reviewing and catching up on information from previous meetings, and leaders are used to it. If left unchecked, it's a surefire way to squelch meeting outcomes.

On the other hand, strategizing comes in last. According to many meeting experts, planning corrective action is not considered strategizing. Proactively working on ways to move the business forward, be it by a team, department, or division, is considered strategizing. Many meeting experts believe that as little as 10 percent of meeting time is spent on strategy.

Case in Point: Former Chairman/ CEO—Large Retail Chain

In an interview, a retired chairman/CEO of this large retail chain expressed his exasperation with meetings. He said that he realized that things were behind schedule. He was frustrated not knowing why. He agreed that the firm had plenty of BI tools to analyze historical performance data, but he felt that they did not address what was occurring with teams in the trenches.

He went on to explain that he would conduct meetings knowing, for example, that out of fifteen initiatives, nine were behind schedule, but he had no idea why. What frustrated him more was the fact that in the meetings, he found team members did not know the answers either. This kicked off a daisy chain of follow-up emails, text messages, and calls that were, in his opinion, frustrating and counterproductive to having the meeting.

He said he would often leave meetings with little or no answers— poor outcomes—and then move on to the next meeting, and the cycle would repeat itself all over again. His goal was to figure out a way to get the debriefing sessions out of the way quickly so that the team could spend much more time on strategic matters.

More to the point, he wanted his finger on the pulse of the business before he entered meetings so that he had a better sense of the status. He lamented, "There must be a better way to manage the business because what we have today just doesn't work."

This CEO is not an isolated case. Numerous senior leaders are frustrated and disoriented when it comes to pinpointing where teams stand at a particular point in time. Many leaders we interviewed claimed to have plenty of BI tools at their disposal to track traditional performance indicators (e.g., revenue, costs, and profits). This is not the problem. What is the problem then?

RULES FOR PRODUCTIVITY

As we know, meetings are the essential communication mechanism for organizations to produce results. They take up much of a leader's time. Conducting productive meetings is a vital leadership skill. The more leaders are armed with solid information prior to conducting meetings, the better the odds of producing good outcomes.

To excel at presiding over meetings takes some basic understanding of workflow dynamics. In the traditional sense, workflow is defined as "the sequence of industrial, administrative, or other processes through which a piece of work passes from initiative to completion." For our purpose, we view workflow from an IW perspective, where their critical activities and the information that they manage comprise the business process.

Far too often, leaders take workflow for granted. They assume teams are cognizant of the workflow processes within the organization. I hate to be the bearer of bad news, but in most situations, this is simply not the case. In a sense, when it comes to improving meeting outcomes, knowledge is power.

Another snapshot tool I designed to help leaders and teams improve meeting outcomes is the Rules of Productivity. Meetings are all about production, as in moving the ball forward. To run productive meetings requires rules that strengthen team dynamics and improve their outcomes. When coaching leaders, I instruct them on how to apply three simple rules:

1. **Preparation**—ready to go.

2. **Participation**—count me in.

3. **Protocol**—stay on track.

Simple as these rules seem, if properly applied, they work well. Time and again, I consulted and coached leaders who have no rules for running meetings. None!

Case in Point: Founder/CEO—Mid-Market Specialty Fabricator

The owner of this Midwest company and an ex-director at PwC has three manufacturing locations and was in the process of acquiring a fourth. His reasoning for the acquisition was simple—extend the breadth of product offering and customer base.

Acting as his strategic advisor, we identified his top three challenges in each of the leadership functions: meeting management, decision-making, and reporting using the Function Assessment Tool.

As always, I started by asking him how he manages meetings and what he thought was the quality of the meeting outcomes. His response: "I run between meetings with little time to address specifics and often leave meetings with less than adequate information to make informed decisions. Then comes the follow-up, which seems to take forever—but that's my life."

This is typical of entrepreneurs who lead high-growth small- and midsize businesses—too much to do and too little time to do it in. Their plight is made that much more difficult when meetings produce less than expected outcomes.

I employed my Rules of Productivity—preparation, participation, and protocol—to help him improve team dynamics and meeting outcomes. Critical to improving outcomes is simplifying the meeting process and adhering to specific rules.

The leadership team was asked to provide their thoughts on how to improve meeting outcomes. After an open discussion, we incorporated their ideas into the three Rules of Productivity. From here, it was easy to get them to understand the power of applying the rules as we incorporated their ideas into the rules.

The good news is that after three months the leadership team estimated their meeting outcomes improved by over 50 percent—that's the results leaders should expect when applying the Rules for Productivity.

This CEO is certainly not alone on an island. Leaders across industries believe that meetings are often underproductive or counterproductive, leaving them frustrated and disoriented as to where teams stand.

Perhaps more disturbing is the fact that team members often share the same sentiments as their leaders, only in spades. Studies have repeatedly shown that over time if meetings continue to be unproductive, it can demoralize teams and lead to poor organizational performance.

Try an experiment. Take a team you lead and have a meeting on meetings. In the meeting, explain the Rules of Productivity. Prior to the meeting, make a short list of characteristics for each rule that you want emphasized. Consider choosing a team that, in your eyes, is marginally productive.

In the meeting, discuss the characteristics selected for each rule. Here is a simple example. Under the rule of participation, list characteristics such as

1. Attend on time.

2. Prepare me for trouble areas.

3. Don't bring problems without solution options.

Engage the team in a discussion about the rules and the desired characteristics. Then, over a predetermined amount of time (for example, one month) send out a tip to team members once a week that applies to each rule where teams continue to underperform. Rate the team and each member by using the following value-based system:

- Market Leader Value

- Significant Value

- Moderate Value

- Little Value

A value assessment system gauges the degree to which someone or something brings value to customers. The system is based on the precepts of Michael Porter, the preeminent Harvard School of Management professor, management consultant, and author of several books on value-based management.

It is used throughout the application of Outcome Dynamics. Stick with the rules. When people break them, let them know. Play the "command" card of leadership to get cooperation. Then, each month for three months, reassess where the team and its individual members stand. There should be noticeable improvement in team dynamics and meeting outcomes.

Preparation

Did you ever notice that certain people are always late for meetings and that their reasons are always the same? Occasionally running late for meetings is to be expected, especially in the on-the-fly workplace of today. However, being habitually late should not be excused, as it has a real impact on meeting outcomes.

In an extensive study published in the *Journal of Behavioral Science* titled "Let's Get This Meeting Started," leading psychologist and organizational expert Joseph Allen says,

> As the number of meetings increases, the quality and value of meetings can have a direct impact on an organization's bottom line in the form of wasted time and effort, not to mention poor morale. Ineffective meetings are a cost that an organization arguably has the greatest opportunity to control.

Allen presents statistical evidence that lateness has a very real negative impact on meeting outcomes, and he claims that leaders can easily control this situation. As mentioned in the What and Why of Focus at the beginning of this chapter, a leader's predominant trait is to command and influence, not to administrate. Getting team members to be on time often requires leaders to play the command card of accountability—be on time!

There was a highly touted study on agile leadership performed by Google in 2019 that concluded, "Expecting individual accountability is part of developing agile leadership qualities." The study explained the importance of leaders to expect accountability on the part of team members, as it is a leader's right and a worker's responsibility. So don't hesitate to use it when appropriate—you have that right.

The Google study dovetails nicely into Allen's findings regarding the importance of punctuality for meetings being seen as accountability. Paraphrasing Allen's conclusion: lateness equates to poor meeting outcomes. This is another example of low-hanging fruit that leaders can focus on to improve meeting outcomes.

Not only is it the responsibility of the worker to be on time, but they must also be prepared to work. In a world where leaders have six to eight minutes to address any one aspect of a challenge within meetings, unprepared participants complicate the job of leaders, given that managing the activity of teams and the critical information that they manage using the fragmented resources of today doesn't work well and getting teams to fully participate in meetings is paramount.

Unfortunately, there is no silver bullet to getting teams to meetings on time. And there is no way to guarantee that teams will be prepared for meetings when they get there, other than pulling the command card and insisting on it. Leaders need to make sure they are doing their part to command the workplace and influence teams to be prepared.

Participation

Once you get teams to attend meetings on time and prepared to work, the next step is to get them to participate in a responsible manner. Many large organizations have project management offices (PMO) that send representatives to meetings to update progress, take notes, assign action items, and the list goes on. But they only do so for matters that meet project management principles and are deemed projects. However, only about 17 percent of the *Fortune* 1000 companies have PMO offices, and almost no small to midsize companies can afford them.

This means that most companies are left to translate projects seen in the IW world as initiatives with no formal tools or techniques to manage them. Many IWs use project management tools when they can to manage the day-to-day business process, but they are not designed for this purpose and therefore fall short of expectations.

Interviewing hundreds of leaders at all levels of the organization, we found that 72 percent believe they struggle to control meeting dynamics and the outcomes. The number one culprit identified was participation. Participation is a critical aspect of producing good outcomes. The need for participation has been significantly heightened with the onset of the pandemic, where managing the business process from a distance has been put into overdrive.

> We found that 72 percent believe they struggle to control meeting dynamics and the outcomes. The number one culprit identified was participation.

In the interview, we alluded to how many resources are available to manage the business process in meetings and suggested that they are not independently built to optimize collaboration, but to augment it. However, do you realize that over 80 percent of leaders and teams still take handwritten notes in meetings? Talk about impeding the democratization of knowledge.

Participants must participate! Good outcomes in meetings depend on it. To unlock the full potential of participation, leaders must once again play the command card. Leaders spend more time wrangling information out of teams in meetings than democratizing the knowledge that is gained in them. This is counterproductive!

Below is another snapshot tool to help leaders manage information flow. Referred to as the Information-to-Action Life Cycle, this simple but powerful tool helps leaders and teams get on the same page and stay there regarding the flow of information.

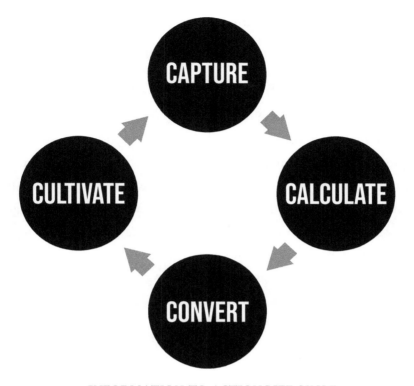

INFORMATION-TO-ACTION LIFE CYCLE

The sequence of steps and definition are as follows:

1. **Capture**—filter in decision.

2. **Calculate**—weigh in decision.

3. **Convert**—include in decision.

4. **Cultivate**—support in decision.

The life cycle represents the steps that information naturally goes through regardless of type or complexity. Each step signifies what leaders do with information at any given point in time. It is the logic that leaders use when they capture, analyze, and share information, whether they realize it or not.

- Decide what information needs to be captured.

- Decide how information weighs into a decision.

- Decide what information plays a part in a decision.

- Decide how to use the information to support a decision.

Applied properly, team members quickly know what leaders want and where information stands in the decision-making process. It promotes a common point of view with a common language to communicate the status of information. It works because humans gravitate to images, and the Information Life Cycle provides an image. Consciously or unconsciously, leaders go through this order of logic when they make daily decisions.

The most important aspect to improving the quality of meetings is participation. If teams don't participate, then why have a meeting in the first place?

Protocol

How leaders conduct meetings can make all the difference in the world. Setting in place a standardized mechanism or protocol to manage meeting dynamics is essential to improving meeting outcomes. There is no set policy or procedure to follow, but rather leaders must decide how they want to run meetings.

The natural tendency of teams is to wander, to go off in directions that interest or involve them individually. This can have a dramatic effect on meeting outcomes. Leaders must know when to play the command card, as it is their responsibility to produce results. After all, it is their meeting.

Far too often, I've observed leaders being led rather than leading. This adds to many team members feeling like meetings are a waste of time, as cited earlier in Allen's study.

This is partly due to leaders wanting to give team members a "share of voice" in the decision process, which in and of itself is a good thing. However, great leaders appear to have a set routine to manage meeting dynamics regardless of the type of meeting. This repeatable routine helps them effectively and efficiently lead meetings.

I recommend that leaders take a bit of time and whiteboard a protocol for running meetings that works best for them and that can easily be communicated to teams. Understand that, with on-the-fly leadership, there is a significant fallout on the amount of time leaders can spend on any one aspect of a challenge. Debriefing alone could eat up to 40 percent of the meeting time. Leaders must take this into consideration when setting protocol.

Leaders should try spending 10 to 15 percent of the allocated meeting time on strategic matters first. Then influence the team to be better prepared to address tactical matters with the remaining time. Influence workforce behavior to be more prepared and participatory.

The road may be a bit bumpy at first; however, you will be surprised by how quickly teams realize that this is the new normal and you are serious and committed to the new protocol. Try three or four different approaches to change up the protocol of running meetings.

Then, after some trial and error, select the protocol that works best for you. Leaders may even find that they can stretch the time spent on strategic matters to 20 percent. You should see marked improvement in team dynamics and meeting outcomes, as I have witnessed working with clients.

Case in Point: Owner/CEO—Online Pharmaceutical Marketing

During a strategy session with me, the CEO of this mid-market technology company shared that he attended a management development program conducted by an outside consulting firm. The moderator started the session by saying that the focus of the program begins with improving meeting management skills.

This took the CEO by surprise. Unfortunately, he said that the program left much to be desired. However, it provided a spark that led him to question how he and his leadership team ran meetings.

He claimed that many of their teams yawned in meetings and saw them as a waste of time. When I asked him whose fault he thought it was, he hesitated, then said, "Mine, I guess!" This scenario is echoed by many leaders. I applied my Rules of Productivity with an emphasis on protocol, as he believed this aspect to be his weakest link.

He flipped the order, starting every meeting with strategic matters. Within three months, he noted,

> I feel stronger as a leader in meetings and the outcomes are measurably better. I stick to a protocol that works. It further improved my ability to convert information into action-able solutions by over 50 percent. Focusing on protocols in meetings has also significantly improved team morale.

This result is not unusual. When teams understand the protocol that meetings will be run under, they tend to adjust, and meeting dynamics take on a new life form. However, it is not a quick fix. It must be revisited and reinforced periodically if leaders are to continue to improve meeting outcomes.

I suggested early on in the chapter that meeting management may be the Achilles' heel of leadership. Indeed, many studies support this claim, a few of which I shared with you. Do not take this leadership function lightly. Meetings are where the democratization of knowledge begins and the collaborative process ignites.

Leaders stand no chance of building the collaborative organization of tomorrow without maximizing meeting outcomes. Since the majority of a leader's time is spent presiding over or participating in meetings, distilling information is as much of an art as it is a science. Practicing how to apply this Morse code-like system is critical to keeping pace.

Presiding over meetings competently and knowing how to get the most out of them is a critical dimension of good leadership. Meetings spark the collaborative process, maximizing performance and moving the organization closer toward excellence.

DECISION-MAKING

The human brain is nothing short of amazing. Even the most powerful computers in the world cannot compare. Computers will never replace the human brain because of reasoning, but it can be a multiplier. Our brains, unlike computers, connect the context of a situation to the semantics, an extremely important aspect of decision-making.

A great example of the human brain in action is in the case of Captain Sullenberger (Sully). He landed a jetliner in the Hudson River just north of New York City in 2009, saving the lives of all the passengers aboard. He did so with brainpower. His brain took over where the aircraft's computers left off. He commanded the cabin and influenced the people onboard to remain calm and confident. He is a true leader!

Yet as organizational life gets more complicated, leaders need help in decision-making that only technology can offer. Deloitte claimed in a 2017 study that "decision-making is a most critical leadership attribute to possess as the world becomes more complex and the number of decisions executives make to respond to market conditions is on the rise." Forrester Research stated in a 2019 study regarding decision-making that "being an 'adroit' decision-maker is a leadership requirement today mostly due to the changing nature of competitiveness."

Especially in the on-the-fly era, quick and accurate decision-making is a prerequisite to good leadership, but the complexity involved is getting out of control, causing many leaders to fear making these decisions. A Korn Ferry study conducted in 2018 concluded, "The capacity of executives to make good decisions that positively impact stakeholders, shareholders, and customers has become cumbersome as complexity worsens and decision-making becomes more multi-dimensional in nature."

Behavior scientists and psychologists agree that leaders have reached a threshold where they can no longer expand their bandwidth to take on more responsibility while maintaining the ability to focus. The inability of leaders to focus their attention is a result of leading on-the-fly. It is a worrisome problem that will be fully addressed in the next chapter.

A Deloitte study published in 2018 titled "Risk Intelligent Decision-Making" states, "The art of leadership and governance is fundamentally about judgment and decision-making" and that "it is possible and necessary that they all share in an understanding of key decision-making skills, processes, and tools." They further suggested that consolidating and integrating the tools and techniques used to manage the business process across the organization is vital to strengthen the decision-making process.

There is no better way of expressing the magnitude of making just a few decisions than was presented in a *Work Design* magazine article authored by Markku Allison in 2019. In it, he says,

Think of this: suppose you have four decisions to make. You can connect those decisions in six possible ways and arrange them in sixty-four possible patterns. If we bump it up just a little, say, to ten decisions, things change: you can connect those ten decisions in forty-five possible ways, but you can arrange them in over 3,500,000 possible patterns. Over 3.5 million! If the sequence of decisions has meaning, that small change in quantity has huge implications in possible outcomes. That's just the tiniest glimpse into the world of complexity.

His depiction of the complexity involved provides a powerful image of what leaders are faced with when making decisions. From his perspective, complexity in decision-making is spinning out of control, and unless it is reined in using data-driven technology, there are many decisions that will never see the light of day.

Companies at the forefront of using data-driven technology to help make decisions are addressing business problems with a whole new mindset. In some cases, they have introduced data-driven business models that have taken entire industries by surprise. Digital forerunners have an enormous competitive advantage, and to keep up with them, incumbents need to apply data and analytics to the fundamentals of their core business while simultaneously applying predictive models to anticipate future moves.

Applying data-driven decision-making is an example of how technology serves the greater good of organizations. Employing them to compete in an increasingly volatile world is necessary, especially in legacy organizations where they have one foot in the past and one foot in the future.

This means using predictive analytic tools to anticipate competitive and market patterns as well as to anticipate performance challenges within existing operations. Leaders today don't have time to ponder decisions as compared to a decade ago. Leaders must react swiftly and decisively. Accuracy in workflow information is a must to accomplish this end.

Streamlining operations, experimenting with new models to enhance organizational dynamics in the way we learn, and sharing information are other critical dynamics in decision-making. The use of predictive analytics to get this job done is unavoidable. Wikipedia defines predictive analytics as "encompassing a variety of statistical techniques from data mining, predictive modeling, and machine learning that analyze current and historical facts to make predictions."

Two of the leading authorities on understanding the application of predictive analytics are CEO Gerhard Pilcher and Jeff Deal, vice president of operations at Elder Research, a recognized leader in data science, machine learning, AI, and an affiliate of our firm.

In their book *Mining Your Own Business,* they lay out the case for why predictive analytics will continue to be transformative, stating, "Organizations that effectively use data analytics undergo a transformation in the way they think. Instead of making decision based exclusively on reports about what has happened, the organization begins to rely on predictions on what is likely to happen and why."

As this is key to understanding where leadership is headed, I quote Pilcher and Deal: "what is likely to happen and why." This is not like going to Las Vegas and placing a bet on the roulette table and watching the wheel spin, hoping for the best. Nor does it mean that the traditional reporting indicators used to gauge the performance of an operation are dead—not by any means.

Predictive analytics relies heavily on historical data to predict the future, and therefore it is extremely important to keep score of current and historical business performance. But the true value of measuring business performance is using historical data to predict the future. Forward-thinking leaders are quickly turning to these tools to guide the way.

There are many decision-making models for leaders to choose from. They come in a variety of sizes and shapes. However, the four shown below are the most widely applied today.

> Instead of making decision based exclusively on reports about what has happened, the organization begins to rely on predictions on what is likely to happen and why.

Decision-Making Models

- Rational decision-making model

- Bounded rationality decision-making model

- Vroom-Yetton Decision-Making Model

- Intuitive decision-making model

If you're not familiar with these models, don't worry about it. Just know that they exist and that they continue to dominate the decision-making landscape. But they are losing their luster. Leaders are turning toward advanced predictive analytic models to help make informed decisions. Predictive analytics adds a whole new dimension to decision-making that enhances the ability of leaders to compete.

Over the next decade, we will see many more technology-driven models that will supersede all that exists. Good leadership going forward requires predicting the future with an acceptable degree of clarity and certainty. As the amount of information required to make decisions rises, so does the time needed to scrutinize information to arrive at an informed decision.

According to Vik Kasturi, founder and president of Digitivity, a highly regarded technology strategy consulting firm serving *Fortune* 500 executives,

> Predictive analytics holds the key for leaders to see the future and anticipate next moves predicted on evidence-based data rather than guesswork. The expanded application of technology in decision-making relies heavily on breakthroughs in AI-enabled automation. This is where we can expect the biggest payoffs from technology to occur.

Kasturi's assertion that AI automation is the ultimate game changer is undisputable. He further believes that "The movement toward the use of predictive analytics to control the direction of performance is a fait accompli, and the first in wins."

Leaders, your time is precious. Decision-making is complex. Adopting advanced analytics tools to help make decisions based on future trends only makes sense. Do this to remain on the forefront of the race to gain the competitive advantage.

Reporting

Since the pandemic put a halt on in-person meetings, the types of reports and the mechanism of reporting have been dramatically impacted. Reporting is obviously a crucial aspect of leadership. Over the last decade, advances made in technology have greatly enhanced—and complicated—this third Core Leadership Function.

Reporting is an account given on a particular matter, especially in the form of an official document, after thorough investigation or consideration by an appointed person or body. Reports can be financial in nature, expressing the value of a company, or they can be operational in nature, where key performance indicators (KPIs) or objective key results (OKR) are used to track progress to goals of an organization. Both are necessary to run the business.

Operational reporting requires leaders to communicate where teams stand to goals. This requires leaders to use detailed data on individual transactions. However, it is often not desirable to maintain data on such a detailed level in the data warehouse due to both the exploding size of the warehouse and the updated frequency needed for operational reports.

However, for line and mid-level leaders, there can be no more important information than detailed data on team progress. They are responsible for how teams perform in driving business results at street level while senior leaders are responsible for how the organization moves to achieve goals. The former drives the latter, but often they are in conflict.

This is the reporting quagmire. Senior leaders need a macro view of the organization while junior leaders need a micro view of teams. The gap between tracking team progress in a department or division and tracking the overall progress of the organization can be immense. This reporting gap is what spawns many of the disconnects, bottle-necks, and voids that we observe today in the collaborative process using fragmented resources for managing systems.

In larger, more complex organizations, reporting is a multitiered activity in which workers report to a line manager, who then reports to mid-level managers, and so on. In start-up or early-stage companies, workers are likely to directly report to senior leaders. Regardless of who is reporting to whom, there are two distinct aspects to reporting: the tools used to report and the techniques used to manage the reporting process.

The old adage "garbage in, garbage out" applies to reporting. Leaders struggle to have the quality of information they need to effectively report. This makes reporting preparation an arduous task, and much of the workforce sees it as a colossal waste of time. Here again, we cite the use of fragmented resources as the primary cause. They are simply inadequate!

Leaders today rely on time-bound reports that contain stale information. This information may be days or weeks old, which disorients and confuses leaders. In a never-fast-enough workplace of tomorrow, leaders can ill afford to spend valuable time preparing to report. Data regarding progress must be streamed live to all those who need it, when they need it, making the reporting process simple.

Leaders, including those at the senior level, like the ex-chairman of the retail chain quoted earlier, are often disoriented as to where teams stand. They want their finger on the pulse of team activity. This chairman knew that things were behind schedule before entering meetings but was in the dark as to why. In meetings, he discovered that his leadership teams didn't know the answers either. This resulted in a daisy chain of follow-ups, which further frustrated this leader.

As was cited earlier in a McKinsey study, leaders have an overabundance of BI tools at their disposal to manage the business process, and they only use a fraction of them. Most of these tools are meant to keep score and do not provide details on where teams stand. The mere fact that leaders have so many tools at their disposal and yet poor performance continues to rise speaks volumes about where organizational life is headed.

The reality of the situation is borne out in our research study "What Makes Leaders Tick," which found that over 60 percent of leaders believe that reporting sessions are often a waste of time. The reasons expressed varied, but the primary reason cited was the time it takes to prepare for reporting sessions compared to the quality of outcomes.

As one senior executive at a major healthcare company said, "I dread reporting because it takes a lot of my precious time to get all the necessary information ready, and it often results in more questions than answers." When leaders can't easily access critical information necessary to report, they get frustrated. This vicious cycle must be eradicated.

For a broader perspective on the function of reporting, I compared Boston Consulting Group, a leading consulting and research firm that concentrates on the analytical side of reporting, against McKinsey, a leading organizational consulting firm that concentrates more on structure and story. While each firm takes a different bent toward reporting, both firms agree that the changing nature of decision-making is having a real effect on the types of reports being generated and the techniques used to manage the reporting process.

These titans of research agree that the transfiguration of reporting underway has moved the focus on the quality and type of information applied and not on the quantity of information produced.

Summary

Leaders command the workplace while influencing the workforce; managers mostly administrate. In either case, overcoming the fallout that leading on-the-fly has on the Core Leadership Functions is mandatory to succeed as a leader.

Leading on-the-fly wreaks havoc across the organization, obliviating the rules of good leadership. No leader, great or otherwise, can escape its reach. Knowing how to contend with the fallout is a critical aspect of good leadership.

The on-the-fly phenomenon requires leaders to adopt a no-detail mentality, which means forming snapshots to keep pace. Progressive leaders will back away from using fragmented resources and seek next generation solutions that simplify, not complicate, the workplace to better manage the business process. The plethora of BI tools have proved to be of little help in tracking where teams stand to goal at any given time disorienting leaders, further adding to their frustration.

FOCUS FACTOR #1

To *outfocus* competitors, leaders must overcome the fallout that on-the-fly leadership has on the Core Leadership Functions in building the collaborative organization of tomorrow.

- Focus on the many ways to improve the skills of commanding the workplace and influencing the workforce.

- Focus on the many ways that viewing excellence as a never-ending pursuit and not as a destination ensures that the organization will continually move forward.

- Focus on adopting as many snapshot tools as possible to counter the effects of leading with a no-detail mentality.

CHAPTER 2

THINGS THAT MATTER

What and Why of Focus

Struggling to keep pace, leaders find it difficult to volitionally focus their attention. Yet leaders instinctively realize that focus is a critical attribute for good leadership. Great leaders want to know *what* to focus on to hone their attention skills and *why* obstacles like leading through immediacy and contending with input overload from teams must not stand in the way.

IN THE FIRST CHAPTER, we learned what the convergence challenge entails and how on-the-fly leadership impacts the Core Leadership Functions. In this chapter, we turn our attention to the blowback effect that on-the-fly leadership has on the ability of leaders to volitionally focus their attention.

Without focus, leaders cannot expect to lead from a strategic position. It's more likely that they will administrate from a tactical position. Being acute of mind is an essential attribute of leaders, to be sure. But the ability of leaders to focus their attention on the things that matter when they matter is a true test of good leadership.

Improving focus necessitates a basic understanding of how the attention management mechanism works. The subject of attention management has several dimensions to it. It has been studied by many branches of science from social scientists to neurologists. By most accounts, it has four dominant aspects: input assimilation, prioritization, judgment formation, and decision-making (a Core Leadership Function).

According to behavioral scientists, the degree to which leaders master this process greatly determines the quality of a leader. Tom Peters, our go-to expert on excellence, expresses it best in his book, *The Excellence Divided,* when he says: "The ability to focus is a critical leadership skill, and selecting the right technology and making the right organizational moves is a crucial part of focus."

To amplify this perspective, I point to a 2017 McKinsey Summary Report stating that "the ability of executives to attend to everything on their plate in a cohesive and timely manner, is to a large extent, no longer possible, causing leaders to pick and choose their battles based on 'immediacy.'" It went on to discuss why leaders have become very tactical by nature, which flies in the face of experts who espouse the virtue of leading from a strategic position.

In 2017, I authored a white paper titled "Simplify Workplace Dynamics—To Supercharge Organizational Performance." One of the exercises in the paper was for leaders to audit the type of work they performed over a week's time and make a list of the work they considered to be low value. Then they were asked to offload as much of the low-value work as possible onto coworkers or eliminate the work altogether.

This exercise can be an eyepopper. Leaders often find that they unconsciously perform many low-value tasks out of habit, not out of necessity. Leaders who reported back claimed they saw a 10 percent to 20 percent uptick in available time to focus on more strategic matters—things that are substantial.

The evidence is overwhelming. Leaders lead by focusing on the most important thing on their plate at any given time, according to the McKinsey study. This tendency to lead through immediacy is confirmed in our findings as well. One senior leader of a major pharmaceutical company quipped, "Strategy is all we talk about but is something we rarely spend time on."

Attention Deficit Syndrome

Evidence in hand, we knew that this condition significantly affected organizational performance and was a force to be reckoned with. To represent this troublesome condition, I coined the term "Attention Deficit Syndrome."

Like any syndrome, there are multiple symptoms that accompany it. We documented dozens of cases where leaders admitted to having unwanted symptoms caused by their inability to focus on the things that matter.

Case in Point: Manager Performance and Quality— Major West Coast Hospital

This leader was in search of a better way to unify the workplace in the research division of a prestigious hospital. His objective was to be a more effective strategic leader. He recognized that workplace complexity was affecting his ability to get things done on his plate so he could move on to more strategic matters.

In a strategy session with him, he shared,

> Our organization is spinning out of control as more responsibility is heaped onto already overburdened shoulders while more technology is introduced to help the worker bees manage their workload. The problem is that more technology causes more confusion and makes my job that much more difficult. Seems like I do more housecleaning than anything else.

He, like millions of leaders, found himself out of breath at the end of the day, flying between meetings and managing through immediacy. Despite his prodigious management background and possessing a Black Belt in Six Sigma, he struggled to keep pace, and he realized it.

Responsible for managing forty to fifty initiatives at any given time, he further admitted that his bigger challenge was getting coworkers to participate and do their part responsibly. He eventually learned to circumvent these coworkers whenever possible, realizing that they were obstructing the collaborative process and diminishing his ability to focus. Admittedly, the avoidance approach was not a long-term solution.

This leader was becoming apathetic toward the workplace. To make matters worse, his world was turned upside down with the pandemic. He was further charged with ensuring that all non-patient-related workers were set up on a work-at-home program.

He bemoaned, "The pandemic only reinforces the need for a solution that consolidates and integrates operating information. Simply leaving well enough alone is no longer an option. Coworkers must contribute and be held accountable, or performance will never improve."

This leader was experiencing the blowback effect of Attention Deficit Syndrome to the max. He had a hard time focusing on the things that mattered. Plus, the wave of resistance constantly pushed back against all his efforts to improve his productivity.

Frustrated and disillusioned trying to keep pace, he sought our help. His plight was not unique but typical. He was leading through immediacy and had lost the ability to think strategically.

We learned the hard way that the subject of focus is more complex than it appears. It's not enough for leaders to simply focus their attention, but it's how they focus their attention that matters most. The key word in describing the quality of focus is "volitionally." The word equates to how one mindfully focuses their attention. For leaders to volitionally focus their attention requires an understanding of the underlying mechanisms of focus when applied in leadership.

Leaders instinctively realize that that they need to control their focus. In our study "What Makes Leaders Tick," we asked over fifty leaders which obstacle out of four options was most detrimental to improving their ability to focus. A whopping 67 percent selected "time" as their number one answer—no surprise there!

Managing one's attention demands that leaders focus on certain stimuli, forcing them to shift their attention away from other tasks. Accomplishing this end is complicated by the wave of resistance pushing against all efforts to improve focus. Recall that attention management is a four-step process: assimilation, prioritization, judgment formation, and decision-making. Mastery over this process is critical to improving focus; however, it also requires a dose of self-regulation.

> It's not enough for leaders to simply focus their attention, but it's how they focus their attention that matters most.

Maura Thomas, a leading educator and lecturer on attention management, defines self-regulation as "The ability to consciously direct your attention in any given moment, to be more proactive than reactive, and to maintain control rather than having it inadvertently relinquished." She goes on to say that "Regaining control over one's attention empowers and makes one more productive and that taking control means knowing how to self-regulate or risk losing control altogether."

No question. There is a direct correlation between how leaders control their attention and their decision-making capability. Given that decision-making comes at the end of the four-step process, it stands to reason that how leaders master the first three steps weighs heavily on the quality of decisions.

This reinforces the need for leaders to improve their attention skills. To accomplish this end, let's examine three widely accepted theories regarding attention management.

Posner Attention Theory

Michael Posner is a leading authority on attention management who many consider to be the father of attention theory. He claims that basic attention theory distinguishes between top-down (endogenous) and bottom-up (exogenous) attention. Bottom-up attention is focused automatically during exposure to salient stimuli.

For example, moving an item in an otherwise still scene is a salient stimulus that will "grab"—that is, focus—bottom-up attention. Top-down attention can be controlled volitionally. Self-control over top-down attention is of central interest to leaders, as it enables them to quickly filter out the things that do not matter. He divides his approach into three categories as shown below.

POSNER MODEL

1. **Alerting Attention**—governs alertness and vigilance, the capacity to sustain attention and be ready to respond to stimuli. It is crucial in activities such as driving, piloting a plane, or monitoring a radar screen as air traffic controllers do.

2. **Orienting Attention**—the capacity to shift attentional focus from one stimulus to another. It is often explained through an analogy to a flashlight beam that can be shifted from one item to the other. It is involved in scanning the environment and selecting stimuli, and it can be either endogenous (top-down, controlled without force) or exogenous (bottom-up, captured by a stimulus).

3. **Attention System**—this is of most interest, as it directly affects executive attention. This system governs the effortful control of attention, such as the decision to ignore some stimuli and focus on others. Some researchers consider all

top-down attention to be executive attention, but executive attention is a more complex system that also includes self-regulation (e.g., the type needed in the process of decision-making).

In Posner's Model, attention system means top-down attention can be controlled volitionally. He explains why acquiring this level of competency first requires competency at the altering and orienting system levels. Leaders who never move beyond the first two skill levels tend to be more reactive and haphazard in their decision-making rather than systematic.

Posner further points out that the level of competency exhibited by an individual is greatly influenced by the type, volume, and quality of stimuli that they contend with over a given length of time. Like all things in life, competency at something requires practice. Mastering how leaders focus their attention is no different.

Nothing draws upon a leader's attention more than the very teams that they manage. This holds true whether it be a single team, a department of teams, or an enterprise full of teams. How teams communicate with leaders greatly influences the attention level required, either positively or negatively. This is no more apparent than when consulting to leadership teams on performance challenges where the stream of mundane tactical inputs crushes leaders' ability to focus.

If the overwhelming volume of input (stimuli) from teams is tactical in nature, then leaders are more likely to apply altering attention and orienting attention rather than attention system, that which is attributed to executives. There is a direct correlation between the different types of stimuli from teams and the application of attention management skills that leaders use to address stimuli.

Posner's top-down and bottom-up theory of attention management is constantly at work. When leaders are bombarded with tactical mundane stimuli every day, it overloads their ability to cope and negates their opportunity to use top-down attention skills when needed. This is the essence of how attention management works, and without understanding the fundamentals, it's impossible to improve attention skills by self-regulation.

Cognitive Load Theory

This theory emerges at the intersection of psychology, education, and communication. The theory explains the cognitive processes involved in learning, and time and again, its worth has been proved. Albeit there are several variations of cognitive load theory, all models are based on the same assumption: the amount of cognitive resource a person can devote to a task at any given time is finite.

This means that leaders have cognitive limitations that break down in a nonlinear proportion over time, impacting their ability to lead. After much experience working with leaders who exhibited symptoms when faced with monumental performance challenges, I realized that there is a point beyond which leaders are no longer effective.

I refer to this point as the Cognitive Breakpoint. I define it as "The point at which a leader's capacity to cope with one or more stimuli, be it tactical or strategic in nature, is no longer possible, as their ability to process information has completely shut down." When leaders reach their Cognitive Breakpoint, they begin to experience a feeling of drowning in information. Their ability to process information spirals downward, interfering with message processing, understanding, memory, and learning.

The cognitive load theory is the basis for most instructional materials targeted at reducing unnecessary cognitive effort to facilitate the learning process in filtering messages. When communicating, messages should facilitate the process, not hamper it. Below is the widely used model developed by Mayer and Moreno depicting how this process occurs.

MAYER AND MORENO'S MODEL

- Selecting information, which involves deciding where to direct attention.

- Organizing material into a coherent mental structure.

- Integrating new material with existing knowledge.

This model is extremely valuable in helping to understand the learning process in converting messages. The ability to communicate and image a message is essential to learning. Given operational levels of sensory perception, the first area where learning can break down between leader and teams is the selection of stimuli commonly known as attention. Deciding where to direct one's attention is the first and most crucial step involved in attention skill improvement through self-regulation.

Realizing that the combination of workplace complexity and work overload contributes to attention deficit and then learning how to self-regulate are crucial steps involved in improving attention skills. A well-constructed approach that helps leaders decide where to direct attention in a coherent mental structure is imperative. This means that the teams that leaders lead must play a role in helping them to self-regulate.

Acknowledging that Attention Deficit Syndrome is real and that all leaders have a Cognitive Breakpoint beyond which messaging, learning, and communication break down begins the process of self-regulation. Improving focus involves getting leaders to know themselves better, which is why it's critical to be aware of the signs and symptoms that they experience just before they hit their breakpoint. This is a vital part of self-regulation.

Executive Attention Management

Everyone needs mentors. They enlighten and provide guidance in some aspect of life. One of my beacons of light was the late Harvard School of Management professor and innovation expert Clayton Christiansen. Many experts believe that Christensen reset the bar for how we approach innovation with his theory of disruptive innovation.

I first embraced Christiansen's leading-edge concepts when I read his book *The Innovator's Dilemma*. His insightful rationale for how the mechanism of innovation works in both theory and practice inspired me and is incorporated in Outcome Dynamics.

Then in his book *The Innovator's Solution*, he introduced the notion that the focus of innovation should be on the "jobs to be done." This premise forces leaders and change agents like me to concentrate on the jobs that customers need or will need to perform to remain competitive on the battlefield of tomorrow.

Simple yet powerful, this perspective further changed our view of the world. We expanded on its application. Before every engagement, we asked ourselves, "What is the job to be done?" This helped clients crystallize the endgame objective and set the direction for our team of consultants. This phrase will be alluded to throughout the book.

A BIT OF HISTORY

Clayton Christiansen and Mark W. Johnson cofounded Innosight, an innovation consulting firm some twenty plus years ago. Since

Christensen's passing, Mark has carried on the consulting legacy. Recently, he coauthored a book with Josh Suskewicz titled *Lead from the Future—How to Turn Visionary Thinking into Breakthrough Growth*.

A provocative and inspiring read, the book puts into perspective the difference between visionary leaders and administrative leaders, or what the book refers to as "Future-Back" versus "Present-Forward" thinking. The book is a must-read for leaders looking to out-position competitors. It changes the markers for how leaders meld vision with action—critical to succeed in the age of collaboration.

I bring Christensen's teachings and Johnson and Suskewicz's book up for two reasons. First, perspective matters! The mindset of leaders affects their ability to focus on the things that matter from C-suite to line managers. A Future-Back mindset can help leaders deal with the devastating effects of Attention Deficit Syndrome, as they are looking over the hill and not caught up in climbing the hill. Second, on many occasions, this book will refer to Christensen as our go-to innovation expert—because he is.

In September 2017, I was invited to join the Gartner Tech Start-Up CEO Program. As the leading global technology research firm, their analysts advise our company in every aspect of operations. One of my key advisors at Gartner was Craig Roth, vice president of market analytics. During a strategy session with him, he shared an experience that he had as part of a Gartner "Maverick" team.

The team was composed of a handful of Gartner analysts who were charged with looking outside the traditional Gartner purview. Together, they discovered that executives faced major issues centered around technology. After much deliberation, the team decided to concentrate on the voluminous amounts of information being generated by technology, viewed by executives as "information overload."

After significant research, the Maverick team published a report titled "The Joy of Information Abundance—And Why Information Overload Is the Wrong Story." It pointed out that "Information work is rapidly approaching a time when noticing relevant information will be as important as making decisions from it." They discovered that executives were looking at the overabundance of information as a negative implication of too much technology.

The Maverick team believed that it was an enterprise-wide problem requiring an enterprise-wide solution. Calling it Enterprise Attention Management, they brought the solution to market. To paraphrase Roth, the approach never got traction for a variety of reasons, not the least of which was the difficulties involved in getting large organizations to adopt an enterprise-wide concept and the fact that they did not have an execution platform to guide the process.

Around the same time, our team was conducting research on the same issue, as it was getting a lot of attention from all corners of the academic and consulting world. Contrary to the Maverick team, we concluded that it was a symptom of the Attention Deficit Syndrome and not a problem in and of itself. This was the true culprit!

Rather than create an enterprise-wide solution to contend with information overload, our firm created a solution that was embedded in the Outcome Dynamics process and could be used independently to help leaders focus their attention. Leveraging the models of Thomas, Posner, and Mayer and Moreno with a heavy emphasis on the cognitive load theory, our solution, called Executive Attention Management (EAM), was birthed. It will be fully discussed in chapter 5.

What and Why of Focus

I can assure you that leadership is as much an art form as it is a science. Great leaders demonstrate an uncanny mastery over their craft. They command workplace dynamics while positively influencing the workforce to move the organization forward. The age-old argument about whether great leaders are born or nurtured continues to haunt experts. Irrespective of one's point of view or the reality of the situation, great leaders rarely come along.

Leadership is a subject that people never seem to get enough of, as evidenced by the fact that over two hundred books have been written on leadership over the last five years alone, according to Amazon. One would think it to be an over-thought, over-theorized, and over-modeled subject if there ever was one. Or is it?

The subject of leadership encompasses an enormous body of work and is an ongoing experiment. Leaders today are the petri dishes to formulate the rules for good leadership tomorrow. However, it is extremely difficult wading through the myriad of theories and models to find much written on the attention management aspect of leadership, especially as it relates to managing the day-to-day business process. It appears that this aspect of leadership is a weak sister within the academic and consulting mainstream, and as a community, we have not done an adequate job communicating its importance to leaders.

Having established that no leader can improve their state in organizational life without honing their attention skills, let's look at how leaders can volition-

> We found that great leaders possess a "sixth sense" about them, being able to look forward and create a vision while at the same time looking back to address the obstacles that can get in the way of achieving a vision.

ally focus their attention on the things that matter, when they matter.

Returning to our study "What Makes Leaders Tick," we found that great leaders possess a "sixth sense" about them, being able to look forward and create a vision while at the same time looking back to address the obstacles that can get in the way of achieving a vision.

We found this to be part of the secret sauce that separates great leaders from merely good leaders. And it relates to the teachings of Christensen and the Johnson and Suskewicz book. Great leaders always have a long-term vision of where they want the organization to go and have a knack for dealing with obstacles that can block the path.

To illustrate how it works, let's examine how two highly regarded authorities, one an organizational theorist and the other a leadership expert, speak to each aspect.

CASE IN POINT: CHAMPY VERSUS MATTSON

- Organizational Theorist Jim Champy presents multiple examples of leaders disrupting markets in various industries in his book *Outsmart!* Champy captivatingly illustrates how these leaders conceptualized, organized, and executed their vision using laser-like focus to make market-altering moves that changed the competitive landscape. Concluding that these leaders used their relentless ability to focus on the vision to gain the competitive advantage, Champy believes the ability to create a vision and see it through to the end is an essential attribute of great leaders.
- On the other hand, David Mattson, president and CEO of Sandler Training and a leadership expert, in his book

The Road to Excellence, warns leaders not to fall prey to the "Blind Spots Syndrome." Leaders are always susceptible to blind spots when running a business. Mattson points out that great leaders know how to identify their blind spots, root them out, and deal with them in the process of achieving a vision. He suggests that knowing why obstacles can derail a vision and knowing how to address them are essential attributes of great leaders.

The uncanny ability of great leaders to effectively do both—create a vision and address obstacles—is what I wanted to bottle. This, I believed, is what separated great leaders from merely good leaders, and I needed a mechanism to illustrate and communicate it to others.

To accomplish this, I created the "What and Why of Focus." This concept is based on the premise that great leaders know how to look forward while looking back. It helps us as consultants to guide the innovation and transformation process. Our professionals use it to keep them on track as they focus their attention on the things that matter in designing and formulating assets of a new or enhanced business model.

At the beginning of each chapter, there is a section called the What and Why of Focus. These sections highlight some aspects of leadership that are found within each chapter.

Case in Point: Division President—
Fortune 10 Technology Company

The president of this $2B solutions division of a high-profile communication company encountered a significant business challenge. Many of the company's hardware patents were on the verge of expiring, and most of the revenue of the division was derived from post-hardware sales consulting.

The chairman of the company was determined to turn the division around. He believed the division was extremely vulnerable to competitors who would enter the business after the patents elapsed, selling their hardware at much lower price points and negating the need for the division's consulting services.

The president confided in me that for years his intent was to swing revenue from post-hardware sales to pre-hardware sales—but procrastination got in the way. Although often discussed at manager meetings, the laser-like focus that this leadership team needed to get the job done, as Champy spoke of in his book, just wasn't there.

I could sense panic. He admitted that he was beginning to detach himself from the workplace, as he had previously tried to make the change using two major consulting firms, but to no avail. It was obvious the pressure that the chairman was putting on this president was driving him closer to his Cognitive Breakpoint.

Enter Outcome Dynamics. As always, we started the process by conducting discover sessions to give their leadership team a chance to weigh in on the current state of the business and suggest ways in which to remedy the situation. Then we asked ourselves, "What is the job to be done?" Once decided, we used the What and Why of Focus to guide the way forward.

In the end, an enhanced business model geared toward pre-hardware sales was launched. It used the same skills, processes, and tools across the enterprise to get the job done. In three years, pre-hardware revenues jumped by 16 percent.

This is an excellent example of a leader who was near his Cognitive Breakpoint. Fact is, he was near his breakpoint even before we met. The lesson learned from this example is that procrastination is the enemy of progress and that leveraging the power of the What and Why of Focus keeps things on track as leaders make changes. Get this right, and you'll have a leg up on becoming a great leader.

Obviously, there are many other characteristics that great leaders possess beyond this one. But none are more important than understanding the application of the What and Why of Focus. Leaders might want to consider adding this snapshot tool to their leadership tool kit.

Telltale Signs

Let's return to the cognitive load theory. Every leader from C-suite to line managers has a Cognitive Breakpoint where information overload creeps in, ultimately affecting understanding, memory, and learning. Behavioral scientists agree that the point at which this occurs varies from person to person, yet it exists in all of us. When leaders begin to reach their breakpoint, their contribution as a leader diminishes in a nonlinear proportion over time.

After working with hundreds of leaders and watching far too many of them struggle with the symptoms of cognitive impairment, we turned our attention to identifying the critical factors involved. This exercise led us to investigate how team input influences the cognitive ability of leaders to lead. After much investigation, we divided team inputs into four factors.

Referred to as the Input Factors, each factor either positively or negatively impacts a leader's cognition. Below are the four Input Factors with corresponding definitions as seen from a leader's perspective.

INPUT FACTORS

- **Complexity**—intricacy of inputs (scored as easy to hard).

- **Volume**—number of inputs (scored as few to many).

- **Quality**—type of inputs (scored as tactical to strategic).

- **Duration**—resolution of inputs (scored as little to too much).

Assessing team Input Factors (stimuli) can be a rude awakening for many leaders. Tracking team input for just one week can speak volumes about the intricacy, number, type, and time spent to resolve an input.

Administering the assessment is simple. Leaders are presented with a scenario and asked to select the option that best represents the impact it would have on their specific circumstances. The objective: to detect patterns in how team input affects the cognitive ability of a leader or leadership team to volitionally focus on the things that matter. Below is a simple example.

Question

Assume you are in the process of year-end planning and some of your team leaders are not responding in a timely manner with their portion of the plan. The clock is ticking, and you are under intense pressure to finish your portion. A team leader who is late with their plan presents you with a complex issue requiring much time and effort on your part to resolve. Which option best represents the impact that this situation would have on your ability to volitionally focus on the issue at hand?

- Major impact

- Significant impact

- Moderate impact

- Little impact

Questions are designed to represent various scenarios coming from different perspectives. Responses are aggregated and plotted on an Input Response Map. Below is a map generated by the Americas division of a $60 billion system integration company.

INPUT RESPONSE MAP

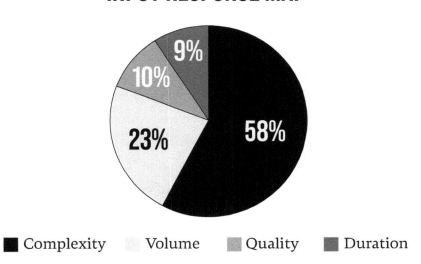

■ Complexity   Volume   ■ Quality   ■ Duration

In this case, the leadership team overwhelmingly believed that complexity (58 percent) had the greatest impact on their ability to focus while volume (23 percent) came in a distant second. The map tells a story of how leaders view input, which then corresponds to the types of attention skills being used to address them. Their attention system skills were stretched to the limit.

Statistically, we found volume to be the number one culprit for producing a negative impact on leaders, forcing leaders to use altering and orienting skills. But here we find that complexity is the problem. Overdoing any of the cognitive skills can lead to stress on the leadership team.

Producing Input Response Maps is an excellent way to identify how leaders view team input, be it for a team, department, division, or an entire enterprise. The objective of the exercise is to categorize team input and identify the cognitive skills that are being used most often and least often.

Understanding how team input influences the cognitive ability of leaders is a crucial aspect of leadership. Yet it is seldom addressed in traditional venues on leadership. An Input Response Map is a powerful weapon to help leaders understand team dynamics from a communication perspective, and it can teach a lot about the dynamics between leaders and teams.

Assessments can be administered as a blind test, where individual anonymity is maintained, or as an open test, where findings are shared across the organization. Historically, we find that open tests are much more effective in producing change in team input. This is another powerful snapshot tool you may want to consider adding to your leadership tool kit.

Case in Point: President—
Large System Integrator

The Americas president of this $60 billion multinational conglomerate was under siege by corporate to grow top-line performance. In our world of innovation and transformation, this meant establishing the current state of the existing business model to determine whether a new or enhanced business model was required.

When we commenced the engagement, this president had already hit his Cognitive Breakpoint dealing with this challenge. He eventually admitted that he found himself overwhelmed and avoided coming to the office. He became apathetic toward the workplace, and he was overcome with a feeling of panic when it came to having to deal with the enormity of the challenge.

As always, we began the process by conducting a few discovery sessions to get the leadership teams take on the current business model and how they would address the performance challenge at hand. Then we asked ourselves, "What is the job to be done?" to center the innovation process. Finally, we applied the What and Why of Focus to guide the entire process.

This was a chaotic workplace. Many teams were disorganized and disoriented. Many others were on the verge of being dysfunctional and in the performance basement. This was a classic example of a company that did not heed the warning signs. Their business model and mode of operation were out of touch with current market and competitive conditions. They were on the precipice of becoming the next Sears, Eastman Kodak, or Motorola.

To better understand the degree to which the leadership team was struggling with team input, we conducted an enterprise-wide assessment. The result can be seen in the Input Response Map illustrated above. Leadership was overwhelmed with the complexity of team inputs.

Why? Because the organization lacked a well-defined business model that could readily compete in a fast-changing market. This circumstance befuddled team members as they received mixed messages from leaders, preempting them to ask what leaders believed were complex questions.

Once a new business model was developed and the assets of the organization were transformed to support it, the communication between leaders and teams was vastly improved. Using the four-step attention management model presented earlier, the leadership team was able to right the ship and find their true north. This enabled the organization to clearly articulate what business they were in, where they fit in the market, and who their direct competitors were.

The firm's top-line revenue increased by over 18 percent in two years. The average contract size increased by over 300 percent. The Input Response Maps played a major role in helping this leadership team get back on track.

Behavioral scientists across the board agree that teams repeat the same input (stimuli) patterns. Unless there is a way to facilitate a change in team input, elevating leaders' cognitive ability to volitionally focus on the things that matter is nearly impossible.

Hitting the Cognitive Breakpoint is unavoidable throughout a leader's career. As leaders reach their breakpoint, they must know the telltale signs before their contribution as a leader diminishes to the point where it crushes any chance of recovery without a change in leadership.

The Pollock Effect

Leaders, listen up! There is no way to improve organizational performance if it doesn't start in meetings. Although the logic behind this assertion was significantly discussed in the first chapter and supported by the findings in the *Harvard Business Review* article and Doodle's report, it cannot be overemphasized.

This is where disconnects, bottlenecks, and voids in the collaborative process go undetected and unresolved. The landslide of changes coming at leaders today is nothing short of breathtaking. The most visible changes can be seen in how we conduct and preside over meetings. With the transition between ages, meetings are taking on new forms.

Meetings will become more purposeful in the future. They will be more strategic versus tactical in nature. They will be steered by humans but driven by technology. And the biggest obstacle standing in the way of presiding over productive meetings is the use of fragmented resources.

To illustrate the effect that fragmented resources have on meetings, I turn to the world of art. Below is one of Jackson Pollock's most famous paintings titled *Autumn Rhythm*. (For those not familiar with Pollock, he was a very successful pop artist in the 1950s). He stunned the art world by inventing what art critics called "action art."

Why the term action art? Because it took many utensils, much footwork, and the flinging of paint onto a canvas lying on the floor to produce a piece. Note from the picture below that there is no central theme to the painting and that the painting consists of a multitude of crisscrossed lines that create a mesmerizing effect.

JACKSON POLLOCK—"AUTUMN RHYTHMS"

Now look at the illustration below. This is a workflow footprint produced for a *Fortune* 100 company taken from a strategy session. Note that when tracing how information is captured, analyzed, and shared in the meeting, there are a multitude of crisscrossed lines, and it takes many fragmented resources (tools) to produce, resulting in an almost mesmerizing effect with no central theme. Hence the term "Pollock Effect" to represent these types of footprints.

POLLOCK EFFECT

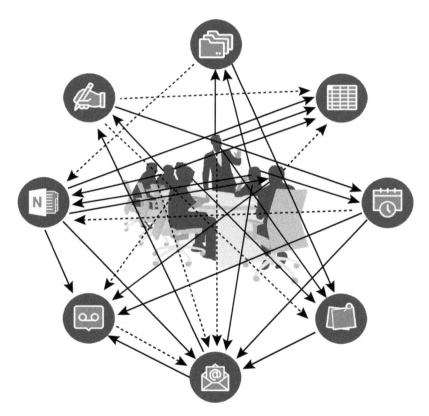

Footprints are generated by auditing the information flow in a meeting. Footprints tell a story about how easy or difficult it is for teams to collaborate in meetings. They reflect the quality of the collaborative process within the organization.

When conducting this exercise, we seek to find where disconnects, bottlenecks, and voids appear in the collaborative process. Notice in this footprint the number of people taking handwritten notes—and what happens to them? Also note the stack of files at the top of the footprint where the session leader, a vice president, kept all his handwritten notes—and what happens to them?

> ## The point is that creating a Pollock Effect is good for art, but it is a disaster for meetings.

The point is that creating a Pollock Effect is good for art, but it is a disaster for meetings. To further demonstrate the impact that using fragmented resources has on meetings, below are side-by-side pictures of what two leaders in a large healthcare organization did with their handwritten notes taken in meetings.

The leader on the left stored her notes in files scattered around the office while the leader on the right converted them to Post-it Notes and then tacked them onto a whiteboard to track progress. Just for a moment, think what this does to the collaborative process.

I'm not suggesting that every meeting generates a Pollock Effect footprint, but far too many do. Nor am I saying that every leader uses manila files or Post-it Notes to manage the business process, yet again, far too many do. Running operations while teams use hand-written notes to manage their portion of the business is not the way to optimize the collaborative process.

In fact, it can lead to organizational suicide. Going forward, self-crafted methods like these will be a thing of the past. Organizations will collaborate on a level never previously imagined, as leaders will have instant access to all that's important in managing the day-to-day business process.

Leaders can't afford to spend valuable time waiting for team members to hunt down critical information stored in the personal folders, tackboards, boxes, and who knows where else. Those days are behind us. At stake is the productivity of leaders and the overall performance of the organization.

Summary

Honing attention skills is a must to contend with the blowback effect of Attention Deficit Syndrome. There are many unwanted symptoms associated with the syndrome, all of which make it difficult, if not impossible, for leaders to volitionally focus their attention on the things that matter, when they matter.

To counter the syndrome, leaders must learn to self-regulate. To get this right, their teams need to be involved. Teams are the primary source of inputs. They must learn how to filter out less important (tactical) matters so that leaders can focus on more important (strategic) matters.

Leaders must master the four-step process of attention management if they want to improve attention skills. Improving the first three steps will automatically improve decision-making. And leaders should know the telltale signs they experience just before hitting their Cognitive Breakpoint where the ability to lead no longer exists.

FOCUS FACTOR #2

To *outfocus* competitors, leaders must hone attention skills to counter the blowback effect that leading on-the-fly has on their ability to volitionally focus on the things that matter.

- Focus on self-regulation using the models of Thomas, Posner, and Mayer and Moreno as guideposts along the way.

- Focus on improving attention management by using the four-step process, knowing that getting the first three steps automatically improves the last step of decision-making.

- Focus on the telltale signs you experience before hitting the Cognitive Breakpoint or risk shutting down as a leader altogether, crushing any hope of improving performance.

CHAPTER 3

LEAN FORWARD

What and Why of Focus

Leaders understand the importance of constantly moving the organization forward. Leaders further understand that the aim is to build an agile organization. Great leaders want to know *what* to focus on to build the organizational structure of tomorrow and *why* obstacles like managing silo structures and matrix management must not stand in the way.

IN THE LAST CHAPTER, we learned how Attention Deficit Syndrome is a blowback effect of leading on-the-fly, which directly impacts leaders' productivity in addressing the convergence challenge. We also discovered several ways that leaders can counter the effects of the syndrome to focus on the things that matter when they matter.

As the steady hand of progress continues to gnaw away at the very fabric of organizational life, leaders must create agile organizations with structures and work systems that are flexible and scalable, the hallmark of a modern organization. In this chapter, we learn about the organizational aspects of the convergence challenge.

In the tug-of-war between the pull of technology and the pull of human resistance, how leaders prepare the human element to adapt to change is a big consideration. To remain on the leading edge of this aspect of organizational life, leaders need to promote a change-ready culture where humans are open and willing to accept the onslaught of changes coming our way.

Throughout the information age, silo structures dominated the corporate landscape. In the age of collaboration, many leaders are tearing down the walls. The topic of open-border structures has finally found its way into the leadership lexicon. But the movement in this direction is proceeding at a snail's pace. The primary reasons? Reward systems and resistance to change.

It's hard to believe that in 2021 many companies are still rigidly managed through silo structures, which will be further explained in chapter five. This mode of operation is a relic. Many of these structures are simply replicas of what competitors use. This best-of-breed mentality does nothing to forge next-generation structures designed to see in your operations what competitors can't in their operations.

Emblematic of the age of collaboration is providing information to those who need it when they need it. This epitomizes the democratization of knowledge, the crucible for success. It is best accomplished through more open-border structures that enable information to flow freely—almost effortlessly—across the ecosystem of the organization.

Archetypes of the open-structure movement can be seen in more entrepreneurial companies. Many of the old-guard companies struggle with this concept due to their reward systems and resistance to change. And to be sure, the importance of having more open-border structures was heightened by the work-at-home craze brought on by the pandemic.

Michael Porter, our go-to expert on value-based management, contends that today "instantaneous equates to competitiveness," and I wholeheartedly agree. I also believe that when it comes to creating the organization of tomorrow, "openness equates to competitiveness." Leaders who move toward open-border structures are the forerunners of building a new generation of organizations unseen and unmatched in history.

Words like "adroit," "nimble," and "swift" are superlatives that management and organization experts use to describe the agile organization. In the never-fast-enough workplace of today, agility, above all other organizational qualities, is required to compete on the battlefield of tomorrow, regardless of industry or size of company.

And without agility, flexibility and scalability are almost meaningless. A 2020 McKinsey report titled "Leading Agile Transformation" states, "This paradigm shift heralds a new form of organization that enables innovation, collaboration, and value creation at unprecedented speed, scale, and impact. Agile organizations can develop products five times faster, make decisions three times faster, and reallocate resources adroitly and quickly." The report goes on to explain why agility is not something an organization trips upon, but something they earn and aspire to.

This begs the question: how does an agile organization differ from the traditional organization? When closely examined, the traditional model evolved primarily with stability in mind, where the business environment and industry sectors being served were predictable. The organization was designed like a great machine with interlocking gears that inched its way toward goals through siloed structures and a hierarchy that rigidly managed operations.

Unfortunately, this gives rise to more structure, more rules, and more control in a world that is becoming less structured, less predictable, and less conforming. In the age of collaboration, leaders must build structures that are more like willow trees that bend with market and competitive winds versus oak trees that remain rigid and unwavering.

Organizations have reached their limit operating under traditional structures. The workforce serving under them feels like they are drowning in organizational complexity and work overload. This tidal wave of resistance pushes against all efforts made by leaders to move the organization forward, testing their resolve.

There are always telltale signs before the fall of a business model. They can be subtle at first, but eventually they become glaring. Good leadership requires leaders to recognize when the model is out of step with market and competitive conditions. The penalty for ignoring the warning signs that a business model is stale and out of touch can be severe.

Stalwart companies such as Sears, Eastman Kodak, and Motorola, once considered beacons of successfully managed companies, have lost their way. However, they didn't lose their way because they didn't have smart leaders but because their leaders ignored all the warning signs that their mode of operation had all but disappeared.

> Stalwart companies such as Sears, Eastman Kodak, and Motorola didn't lose their way because they didn't have smart leaders but because their leaders ignored all the warning signs that their mode of operation had all but disappeared.

The ability to recognize the warning signs that a business model has "gone bad" is a crucial aspect of leadership. Not heeding the warning signs swiftly can be disastrous. With the pace of change today, it's safe to expect many more highly regarded companies to follow suit in the decades to come.

Building an agile organization is the objective. Structures supporting the business model must encourage collaboration through worker participation. Properly conceived, they will eliminate or drastically reduce the disconnects, bottlenecks, and voids found in the process of producing results. Reducing friction in how we collaborate is fundamental in optimizing the collaborative process.

Chaos in the House

The wave of resistance is relentless. Over time, it can build into a tsunami that overwhelms and drowns the workplace. When this occurs, chaos worsens as leaders become more frustrated and disoriented. Workforce morale deteriorates, and workers begin to think about their options, like jumping ship. Righting this situation is difficult at best, and in many cases it's downright impossible without new leadership.

Much scholarly work has been conducted on the workplace and its impact on the workforce. There are a couple of points they agree on:

- Workplace complexity and work overload are on the rise and have a direct impact on organizational performance.

- Over time, a chaotic workplace will not only degrade the performance of the organization but denigrate the culture of the organization.

Peter Drucker, proclaimed the management guru of the century by the *New York Times*, repeatedly reminded us, "Chaos is an opportunity, not a threat." He touted this belief over his fifty-plus-year career. He sincerely believed that turning chaos into opportunity was a sign of a great leader. He proved time and again that this was the case. But are things changing? Is the current paradigm shift different?

As the proliferation of technology continues to make the workplace an ever more complex environment to get things done, chaos creeps in. To an extent, all companies experience a certain level of chaos, but it is usually manageable. In fact, I daresay that leading in a chaotic environment is more prevalent today than ever before, and it wears on the human spirit. Contending with the convergence challenge when chaos reigns supreme in the workplace is much trickier but more needed.

I believe Drucker is correct. Great leaders will rise above the fray, turning chaos into opportunity to gain the competitive advantage. That is something you can count on.

Case in Point: Founder/CEO—Pharmaceutical Internet Marketing

The founder of this privately held high-growth internet marketing company serving the pharmaceutical industry recognized early on the upside potential in a market niche. His firm was the first to succeed at marketing a pharmaceutical branded drug called Claritin online directly to consumers. The company's success with Claritin received much acclaim, and they remained the market leader in this area for several years.

Then competitors appeared on the scene in droves. The founder's vision to future success was blurred. He saw nothing but chaos in the market, and he was looking for a way to turn chaos into opportunity. After two unsuccessful tries with major consulting firms, he turned to Outcome Dynamics.

As always, we conducted discovery sessions with their leadership team to get a take on how they viewed the performance challenge and what their proposed solutions would be and sealed them away. Then, we asked ourselves, "What is the job to be done?" and decided that a new business model was the only prudent course of action. Finally, we used the What and Why of Focus to guide the innovation process.

To be blunt, what we found was a business model that had run its course. The firm was competing in the "dark space" of the market where it is difficult to differentiate value, there is no price elasticity, and little room for growth. When a business model declines to this point, leadership teams see nothing but chaos.

After applying Outcome Dynamics, a new business model emerged with more open-border structures. The new structures enabled the firm to be more adroit, nimble, and swift to react to fluid market and competitive conditions. Furthermore, the structures encouraged workers to easily participate in the collaborative process and be more engaged in contributing value to results.

With the new business model, the company won the Internet Marketing Company of the Year award, and the founder was awarded CEO of the Year by the pharmaceutical marketing industry. This is an example of a leader that relentlessly pursued a course of action to turn chaos in the market into an opportunity for his firm—and it worked!

When the workplace becomes chaotic, there are usually many factors at play, and none are more contributory than the sheer volume of workflow. Work overload is a direct result of an overabundance of workflow. When the volume of workflow exceeds the human capacity to cope, chaos creeps in.

A major study that amplifies how the volume of workflow alone can lead to chaos in the workplace was published in the *Journal of Organizational Behavior* in 2020. Titled "Dynamic Patterns of Flow in the Workplace," it concluded the following:

1. Flow in the workplace represents a high degree of within-individual (pertaining to self) variables characterized as chaotic in 75 percent of the cases studied.

2. High levels of flow are associated with chaos.

3. Different levels of the flow experience seen as merging of actions, awareness, age, and job type are associated with the emergence of different, often unwanted patterns (e.g., chaotic, random).

This study, like so many others on workplace and workforce dynamics, leaves little doubt that the volume of workflow alone is enough to turn the workplace into chaos. This causes leaders to feel overwhelmed—drowning, if you will, trying to keep pace.

The study also showed that the longer chaos persists in the workplace, the more performance worsens. A senior executive of a healthcare client who was experiencing a great deal of chaos in his division may have said it best when he declared, "We have chaos in the house."

While discussing how the proliferation of technology contributes to chaos in the workplace with the late Pete Bradshaw, president of Organizational Consultants Inc., School of Organizational Management professor at the University of North Carolina, and an adjunct consultant to our firm, he shared, "A primary cause of the chaotic workplace of today comes from work overload. Executives are using technology as a weapon to reduce headcount that to a great extent is responsible for the uptick in workload. Over time, employees become less productive, crushing organizational performance."

I, too, have witnessed leaders who use technology to justify contracting the rubber band of resources, thinking that it alone will enable the organization to do more with less. Assessing the return on human capital periodically is good and necessary. However, as leaders squeeze down the workforce, just realize that the volume of workload increases proportionally on the remaining workers. The attitude of "do more with less" has a limit.

Power of the Hammer

Managing through matrixes is nothing new. For decades, large companies have used grids for dual reporting structures. It usually reflects the complexities of their business. But as we will see, managing through matrixes can further complicate the workplace and become a barrier to optimizing the collaborative process.

Because there are distinct benefits of a matrix-run organization, leaders will not be going back to conventional "org charts" any time soon. But the problem is that a matrix will breed and multiply. Some companies even operate with four to six different matrixes simultaneously. With so many dotted lines going in every direction, the authority of leaders to get a job done is diluted.

Working in matrix structures, leaders often find themselves in need of workers who report directly to other leaders to complete initiatives. In these situations, leaders do not own the "hammer" to command workers to get the job done, which adds to their frustration.

The incentives and penalties that their counterparts deal with in less traditional organizations place them at a competitive disadvantage. Leading without the hammer can be disconcerting to many leaders and counterproductive to optimizing the collaborative process.

Matrix-managed organizations are usually found in large legacy companies with roots that go back several decades. Leaders in these companies have a harder row to hoe in building the agile organization of tomorrow, as matrix structures impede the collaborative process. Leaders competing under matrix-managed companies find themselves between a rock and hard place, as they are responsible for getting the job done without the hammer.

Case in Point: Clinical Director— Major East Coast Hospital

A division director in this community hospital wanted to improve how teams collaborated to maximize performance. As a large institution, it used matrixes to manage operations. Many of the director's initiatives required cooperation from team members that did not directly report to him, as they had a dotted-line reporting relationship.

According to many reliable sources in the hospital, the workplace had become very chaotic. The need to do more with less seemed to be the mission of the hospital from the top down. There were signs everywhere that workplace complexity and work overload were crushing morale and affecting the performance of the division within the hospital.

However, the inability of this leader to get everyone on the same page and keep them there while going through the transformation process got the best of the director. Without the hammer to control team dynamics, the director eventually succumbed to team pressure, and the initiative ground to a halt.

Not often, but occasionally, I have seen this situation play itself out in matrix organizations. The hurdle of not owning the hammer is so insurmountable that the job of transformation never gets done.

Cross-Functional Cooperation

Another trend that flies in the face of building an agile organization is the growth of cross-functional initiatives in matrix-managed organizations. Cross-functional initiatives are not only growing at an incredible rate, but they are also more complicated than previously thought, according to many leading research authorities.

These studies show cooperative team behavior as the number one reason for late or incomplete initiatives in matrix-managed companies. The lack of cooperation is precisely what occurred in the example above with the division director at the hospital.

One of the main issues with the matrix approach is that leaders who are responsible for goals don't always own the hammer to ensure cooperation between team members during execution. This raises the following question: How do leaders create agility in matrix-run organizations given that cross-functional initiatives are on the rise and are more complex than originally thought?

This is a tough challenge with no simple answer. Leaders attempting to bring agility to a matrix-managed organization must receive cooperation from workers. History tells us that whenever there is a problem to be solved, there will be solutions forthcoming, but voices must also be heard.

Structures in matrix-run organizations are always silo-based. The reward systems that support them do not work well in the modern era, which will be fully explained in chapter five. To move an organization forward in a matrix-managed environment, leaders need to be creative and rethink ways to achieve greater team cooperation.

Conventional wisdom will not work. This is not an easy challenge to overcome. But great leaders will find ways to turn the chaos of managing cross-functional initiatives without the hammer in a matrix organization into an opportunity to gain the competitive advantage.

Structures That Work

Fundamental to creating an agile organization is building structures that can quickly react to market and competitive conditions. In the process of building structures, customers must remain center stage. I cannot recall a time in a discovery session held at the beginning of each consulting engagement when the leadership team didn't believe that they were customer-centric, customer-focused, customer-friendly—and the metaphors roll on.

To varying degrees, we found this to be the case. However, when leaders are asked to provide the logic for their opinion, we often find that teams were out of sync. Gauging how leadership teams view customers and how the business model serves customers goes a long way toward understanding the logic of the existing structures.

Let's put another stake in the ground. Customers drive structures. Structures that work well serve customers well. This may make a whole lot of sense in theory, but in practice there are a host of hurdles that get in the way. Nonetheless, placing customers center stage when re-architecting structures will ensure they better serve customers in the end—and isn't that the intent?

In our world, an organization that accomplishes this is referred to as being customer-connected. Not just another metaphor, it requires the application of our proprietary system to get there. The term aptly depicts how the system connects the dots between value produced and the logic customers use to perceive value—from a jet plane to a pencil!

> Placing customers center stage when re-architecting structures will ensure they better serve customers in the end—and isn't that the intent?

On the way to building open, inclusive, and nonhierarchical structures that continually evolve to better serve customers, leaders must build customer-connected cultures. Great leaders will ensure that everyone, and I mean everyone, in the organization understands the What and Why of Focus as it relates to customers. And they will insist that it permeates throughout the culture of the organization.

Many senior leaders assume that their leadership team is in lockstep on how they view customers and how the business model serves customers. They are often shocked when they discover that teams are not on the same page in this regard. We found this to be commonplace when conducting discovery sessions in client organizations.

Case in Point: CEO—Manufacturing Software Company

This CEO was a veteran of turnarounds. He was at the helm of a long-standing technology company that provided manufacturing and logistics software. The board was peppered with high-profile Wall Street firms. The company was doing $60 million in revenue, and the board wanted it sold or merged. After a few failed attempts to accomplish this objective, the CEO engaged our firm to help get the job done.

As always, we conducted discover sessions at the beginning of the engagement. The leadership team consisted of twenty-seven people. One exercise in our discovery process was to have leaders privately write down the answers to three questions:

1. What business are you in?

2. What is your view of customers?

3. What is your solution to the performance challenge at hand?

The exercise, although fun at times, is extremely valuable to set the stage for innovation and transformation, yet it can be a senior leader's worst nightmare. The answers to the first two questions are openly discussed in sessions. The third question regarding their opinion of a solution to the performance challenge is locked away until the final solution is revealed.

In my post-session debriefing with the CEO, he was surprised to learn in the discovery session that the leadership team had such diverse views of how the business model served customers. He exclaimed, "This situation is like the book *Men Are from Mars, Women Are from Venus.* My executive team seems to be on different planets." The sessions revealed a disjointed leadership team that had dramatically differing views of the business.

With the current business model, they were competing in the "dark space" of the market with little differentiation, no price elasticity, and no potential for rapid growth. This set the tone for innovating a new business model, as there was no way to enhance the existing model.

Applying the What and Why of Focus to guide our process, the new model that emerged required a complete redesign of the structures to support it. Flexible and scalable work systems were created to ensure that the company exhibited the attributes of an agile organization. The result of our efforts was a business model that redefined the parameters to get the job done. It was a truly disruptive model in the market.

Heralded as a significant breakthrough in the manufacturing software sector by the likes of PwC, Deloitte, and Gartner, the company went on to achieve new heights. Featured in several podcasts and high-profile business and industry magazines, the company was sold to a large competitor for over $60 million within two years.

In a *Wall Street Journal* interview, the CEO claimed that "about 70 percent of the deal was consummated based on the new business model that attracted larger customers at higher price points which required less resources to deliver."

This is an excellent example of the vast difference in how leaders in the same company viewed customers. The difference between how senior leaders perceive business models serving customers and the rest of the leadership team can be dramatic and costly.

Upon innovating a new business model and ending our engagement, we opened the hermetically sealed envelope that contained the recommendations from the leadership team. This is where the fun began! One by one, we exposed the solution submitted by each leader—without naming names, of course. One by one, leaders owned up to the solution that they submitted. Teams found this last exercise to be rather humorous and, in some cases, downright hilarious, looking back and comparing.

However, it served a higher purpose. Discovery sessions are based on system theory. It asserts that organizations, seen as open social systems, must interact with their environments to survive. Every system is bounded by space and time, influenced by its environment, defined by its structure and purpose, and expressed through its functioning. It's a bit like the adage "The whole is greater than the sum of its parts."

Drawing upon the theory, discovery sessions are a series of game-like vignettes that innocuously uncover organization and leadership dynamics. Peeling back specific aspects of how leaders lead layer by layer is immensely helpful to everyone—consultants and leaders alike—to understand the total organizational picture.

Discovery sessions are a fixed part of Outcome Dynamics. However, it is also offered as a stand-alone consulting service. Conducting these sessions can be very beneficial to jump-start the efforts of the do-it-yourself leaders who prefer to move the organization forward using internal resources (to inquire about this service, please visit whitespacellc.com and click on the "Services" tab).

Customer-Connected Culture

In the world of transformation, consultants look at the three dimensions of the organization to enact change: people, process, and technology. These three pillars of performance are the foundation upon which many change programs are based. Note that two out of the three pillars are part of the convergence challenge: people and technology.

The presumption is that by concentrating on these areas of the organization while enacting change, you dramatically increase the odds that organizational performance will improve. Conversely, we view the three pillars as part of a larger group of asset categories that are equally important and must be addressed at the same time.

Moreover, the three pillars say nothing about how customers factor into re-architecting the structures that support a business model. We have firmly established that the creation of structures that better serve customers is incredibly important to move the organization forward.

Placing customers center stage throughout the innovation and transformation process is paramount. Finding that traditional mechanisms were sorely lacking to get the job done, we invented a next-generation system that ensures customers remain at the center of the universe while structures are being designed.

Called the Value Component System (VCS), it is used to quickly deconstruct the asset composition of existing structures and reconstruct the asset composition of the structures to better serve customers. The secret sauce to the system's success fully depends on how it automatically connects the dots between value produced and value perceived by customers.

Below are the asset categories (nicknamed the "Six Ps") that every company in every industry uses to produce value for customers. Convinced that the Six Ps approach worked, we offered a one-thousand-dollar reward to any leader who could identify an asset that produces value for customers that does not fit into one of the asset categories. After twenty years of offering the reward to hundreds of leaders in client organizations, no one has been able to pierce this bulletproof approach, albeit many gallant attempts have been made.

ASSET CATEGORIES

- People—humans that support structures.

- Products—products/services that support structures.

- Procedures—work systems that support structures.

- Policies—processes that support structures.

- Property—property (intellectual and real) that support structures.

- Price–costs to support structures

On the flip side, below you'll find the four value components that customers use to assess value in making a purchase. Note that the order in which they are presented is the order of logic that customers use to assess value before making a purchase.

- Start Value—the "*wow*" factor to gain customer interest.

- Identity Value—the brand, positioning, and messaging to customers.

- Impact Value—the affect or effect on customer performance.

- Relationship Value—the customer life cycle experience.

Below is a value construction template used to deconstruct and reconstruct a business model. Note that the formation of company assets is directly connected to the customers' logic of purchase.

VALUE CONSTRUCTION TEMPLATE

	Start Value	Identity Value	Impact Value	Relationship Value
People				
Products				
Procedures				
Policies				
Property				
Price				

The tool we developed to assess how assets perform is called Value Dynamics Testing. This simple yet powerful tool provides insight into how customers resonate to various aspects of value found in a product or service. Let's see how it works.

Participants are posed with a series of questions. Out of four options, they are asked to select the one option that best represents the degree to which they perceive value for each question. The four options that participants select from are shown below.

- Market Leader= 4 points.

- Significant Value= 3 points.

- Moderate Value= 2 points.

- Little Value= 1 point.

The scores are scribed and tallied on a Value Dynamics Scorecard as shown below.

VALUE DYNAMICS SCORECARD

	Little Value 1	Moderate Value 2	Significant Value 3	Market Leader 4
People				
Products				
Procedures				
Policies				
Property				
Price				

The scorecard tells a story about customers' perceived value. The insight gained from running these tests can be substantial. Leaders can see clearly where assets need to be modified, added, or deleted. The system enables leaders to see the bigger picture and make the appropriate adjustments in the work systems that support structures to better serve customers.

Scoring is straightforward. Let's assume the VP tests 10 aspects of recruiting executives. A perfect score then would be 40 (10 questions x 10 market leader responses worth 4 points each = 40). Certainly, if the results come back considerably less than desired, the VP should consider reformulating the asset competition once again and then retest.

VCS contains a series of templates, but these two alone can help leaders. When applied, leaders are looking to maximize organizational performance by reformulating assets that support structures. However, it also improves the collaborative process by eliminating many of the disconnects, bottlenecks, and voids found in connecting value produced to customer expectations.

VCS can be universally applied regardless of industry or size of the organization. Leaders may want to consider adding these snapshot tools to their leadership tool kit (to receive the entire VCS series of templates visit our website at whitespacellc.com and request a kit).

Agile Qualities Matter

Since building agile organizations is a requirement to stay competitive in the age of collaboration, then it only makes sense that leaders who develop agile qualities themselves will be more effective leaders and have a leg up on becoming a great leader. And never forget that there is no better way to recruit followers than to lead by example!

However, several of these qualities are the antithesis of what we see in many organizations. This is especially true in large legacy organizations where mottos like "stay the course" or "don't rock the boat" echo throughout the halls. As we move along the collaboration journey, leaders must be willing to "think outside the box" and "push the envelope" if they are to lead the organizations of tomorrow.

Over several interviews with Barbara Miller, former VP of global sourcing and data management at AmerisourceBergen, a *Fortune* 10 pharmaceutical distribution company, regarding the state of affairs leading in large legacy companies, she quipped, "Agility, in the pure sense of the word, is extremely difficult in large multinational companies. Many of them have reached a critical mass threshold that will not allow them to compete under the same structures and rules that made them the behemoths that they have become."

I found Miller's sensibility regarding the challenges that multinational companies face as the world order continues to be challenged by smaller, more forward-thinking organizations to be captivating. She went on to say,

> Recognize that size, although the name of the game, from a competitive position can be and usually is a hindrance from an organization efficiency perspective. I daresay much of the inefficiencies that occur daily are simply glossed over by the magnitude of a company, and therein lies the inability of senior leaders to see the need to adopt more agile qualities.

Developing agile qualities begins by learning how to guide and support rather than direct and micromanage teams. The requirements to develop agile qualities were accentuated in a well-respected research study conducted by Google in 2019. It showed that "creating a sense of psychological safety, where people feel comfortable, speak openly suggesting ideas, and admitting they don't know, was one of the pervasive characteristics of high-performing teams." It goes on to explain that "managers will need to create this environment by encouraging everyone to contribute, facilitate joint problem-solving, and encourage team members to take accountability for individual and team outcomes."

Encouraging inclusiveness in the workplace is a critical aspect of influencing workforce participation. However, the study goes on to suggest that supporting self-reliance, encouraging idea creation, and tolerating risk are crucial qualities of agile leaders.

The Google study further showed that leaders should encourage team members to be accountable for their individual contributions. This is a performance game changer if leaders get it right. I have repeatedly heard leaders complain about the lack of accountability when it comes to workers getting things done with a sense of urgency.

Many performance experts believe that the lack of accountability is a major barrier to improving organizational performance, and it can certainly impact the collaborative process. In matrix-managed organizations where leaders do not own the hammer over all team members, they are often left to their own guile to get cooperation.

Accountability has many dimensions. This aspect of building agile qualities cannot be overemphasized, as the majority of employees need to get better about taking responsibility. Regardless of structure, if coworkers are not held accountable, failure to meet goals is inevitable. Furthermore, accountability plays a major role in collaboration.

Collaboration depends on individual coworkers responsibly participating in the collaborative process, and collaboration on initiatives is only as good as its weakest link. Since the pandemic, leaders have been dedicating a lot of time working on managing the business at a distance while relying heavily on individuals to do their part, and who knows if or when the workforce will return to the henhouse.

Perhaps more intriguing is how agile leaders embrace uncertainty and ambiguity with greater confidence. The confidence to take on the unknown is vital to succeed in an unstable world. Examples of this level of confidence can be seen in organizations like Amazon Prime in package delivery, Harry's in razor blades, Uber in transportation, and Tesla in the automotive industry.

> Collaboration depends on individual coworkers responsibly participating in the collaborative process, and collaboration on initiatives is only as good as its weakest link.

When we look closely at companies of this nature, we see leaders who thrive on uncertainty and ambiguity. Dealing with ambiguity is mandatory for survival in an age when the competitive landscape of industries is being reshaped almost daily.

Albeit addressing ambiguity has never been high on the leadership curriculum in the past, things are changing rapidly. Tolerance for risk-taking is becoming a rule for good leadership. Foretelling the future and taking measured risks to move the organization forward is symbolic of the paradigm shift.

Factoring ambiguity into the leadership equation is essential. Referring to Tom Peters once again, he claims, "Leadership in the twenty-first century AD is exactly what it was in the twenty-first century BC. Nothing has changed. Leadership is influence."

Great leaders get it. They understand that possessing agile skills is not an option but a requirement to lead in the modern era. This quality matters when influencing the workforce and building an agile organization with leaders who possess agile qualities is a modern leadership trend.

Drag On Performance

To make the transition between ages a bit more challenging, IWs, the fastest growing segment of the workforce, will greatly impact the ability of the organization to collaborate. Defined by Wikipedia as "Individuals who create, manage, share, receive and use information in the course of their daily work, including those who act and react to information," IWs hold the most promise to move the needle on collaboration.

Without IWs buy-in and participation, optimizing the collaborative process is nearly impossible. IWs have been shown to be the greatest drag on performance. As cited in chapter one, they dominate the landscape of organizational life and are the primary cause of poor performance.

To get a sense of the scale of the IW population, I turn to calculations made by Foundational Inc., a sell-side advisory and analytics firm headquartered in Manhattan's Financial District and a strategic partner of our firm. The company's founder/director, Harlan Milkove, leveraged his firm's in-depth understanding of analytics to determine their numbers.

To address the challenge, they calculated that there are approximately 35.6 million IWs that work for *Fortune* 1000 companies. The firm based this amount on LinkedIn's reported number of *Fortune* 500 profiles that they claim represent approximately 25 percent of the total *Fortune* 500 population (35.6 x 25%/1000 = 8,900 employees).

So on average, every *Fortune* 1000 company has at least eight to nine thousand IWs, which should relay to all leaders that IWs are a force to be reckoned with. Beyond that, the US Bureau of Labor and Statistics predicts that IWs will grow at an annual average rate of 13.7 percent through 2024. Obviously, these are startling numbers, and therein lies the reason that leaders must heavily focus on this segment of the workforce.

To further complicate matters, managing IWs has proved to be more difficult than expected. According to management experts, IWs prefer a level of autonomy and do not like being overseen or managed. To an extent, this flies in the face of optimizing the collaborative process.

Those who manage IWs are often IWs themselves or have been in the past. Activities must be carefully considered before assigning a manager to an IW, as their interests may not be aligned with others, which inevitably will affect the completed work quality, especially in matrix-based companies.

IWs want individuality and autonomy in the workplace. Individuality is an important human consideration on the micro level, but it can hamper the ability of teams to effectively collaborate on a macro level. Finding the right balance between individuality and team participation among IWs is another aspect of good leadership.

Perhaps more interesting is that IWs are the caretakers of critical information that leaders need to perform Core Leadership Functions. Using a hodgepodge of fragmented resources, IWs find it difficult to retrieve and share information seamlessly. This often leaves leaders in the dark as to where teams stand in the process of producing results.

Unlike traditional project management applications where a systematic methodology and specialized tools are used to address the tasks involved in a project, IWs are left to fend for themselves. Performing hundreds of diverse and disjointed activities, IWs are left to their own devices, using an array of fragmented resources to manage their part of the process. This puts an enormous drag on performance.

Borne out by the results of our research and experience, there is no question that IWs add to the burden involved in leaders trying to keep pace. Using a mishmash of resources to manage the business process at street level has proved to be a formula for disappointment. This is unsustainable as the transition between ages relentlessly places pressure on leaders to do more with less.

Optimizing the collaborative process depends on how well IWs adjust to an ever-changing workplace. A certain level of independence in the workplace is acceptable if IWs can responsibly contribute value to producing results. To optimize collaboration, IWs must be provided with state-of-the-time tools and techniques to help them get their job done.

Bottom-Up Participation

To help move an organization forward, leaders typically turn to Learning and Development (L&D). In the world of L&D, leaders use knowledge sharing as a way to mold organizational culture through education dedicated to IWs.

Over the last several years, there has been a predominant shift in how knowledge sharing is viewed and accomplished. For decades, a few people, often in the human resource department, decided what to teach and when to teach it, pushing content down through the organization and assuming learning would occur.

In today's digital world, this approach has been turned on its head. Content moves from the bottom up and is no longer about the pedigree of information but how the information is disseminated between leaders and teams. Much of this aspect of organizational life relates to chapter two, where we discussed how team input directly affects the cognitive ability of leaders to cope.

Many L&D experts agree that the shift from top-down to bottom-up learning is part and parcel of the collaborative movement.

There is consensus among these experts that knowledge sharing builds organizational strength, which is vital to remain competitive. Everyone, especially senior operating leaders, wants to measure the results (who learned what and how much), and there are plenty of measurement tools available to assess team progress.

In fact, the classic return of investment (ROI) model for L&D is being augmented through the mining of operational performance data. This technology serves the greater good of the organization. Leaders can now detect issues such as process/standard operating procedure (SOP) inefficiencies and identify teams or individuals who exhibit suboptimal performance compared to industry or business segment benchmarks.

Line managers to senior leaders need this capability to gauge operational performance in real time. Leaders can view a situation and intervene immediately to mitigate and remedy performance problems. These trends are emerging quickly as every aspect of work continues to be redefined: where we work, how we work, who we work with. Everything is subject to change as advances in technology continue to challenge the status quo.

However, pushing against the forward progress in L&D is the continued practice of hiring out-of-the-box leaders. According to Randy Samsel, founder and CEO of eSearch Talent Solutions and a leading authority in this area, "The job market at executive levels is inefficient. Hiring managers who have been trained to look for résumés that match their skill-heavy job descriptions. The mindset of hiring leaders whose background checks all the boxes in the job description is questionable at best."

While this approach seems logical, it can be shortsighted. After years of experience working with senior hiring managers, Samsel believes that finding good talent is not about recruiting leaders that can hit the ground running in the short term, but about finding the right individual to lead the way forward long term.

Great L&D leaders understand the significance of helping operating leaders acquire the right talent to get a job done, not the right résumé to check all the boxes. I, too, have seen the "résumé buy" win out over the "right buy" time and again. Seldom does it work out long term. It usually causes more consternation among coworkers than it's worth, not to mention the replacement cost.

To promote worker participation from a human resource perspective requires that IWs become a more productive part of the collaborative process. This begins by hiring the right leaders. Miss the mark on this one and watch how quickly the collaborative process and employee performance spiral downward.

To candidates looking for positions, Samsel suggests, "Rather than trying to convince hiring managers that you do check all the boxes, focus on offering up what you can do that every organization needs—mastery over core leadership skills, possessing agile qualities, and a penchant to deal with ambiguity."

Overwhelmingly, leaders hire smart people who have the right knowledge and know the best ways to keep the business in its most successful state. But do leaders have programs in place to identify high performers? Possessing the right talent in an organization is one thing; identifying and nurturing talent to optimize collaboration and maximize performance is something else.

Prior to starting an engagement, Samsel sets the stage by sharing his insight: the hiring managers' job is to help the organization to identify, attract, and hire the best talent to succeed now and in the future. This is akin to our approach of asking "What is the job to be done?"

He begins the process by asking two simple questions:

1. How is your company different today compared to five years ago? From even last year, given COVID, social changes, supply chain interruptions, etc.?

2. Will your company be the same as today in five years or fewer?

According to Samsel, these questions lead to lively discussions concerning what a company has been and will be experiencing. He says to hiring managers, "Perfectly matched candidates may or may not be able to adapt. Wouldn't you be better served by hiring candidates with relevant skills, excellent leadership qualities, and the ability to demonstrate adaptability?"

His role as a thought leader is to reset the bar by which hiring managers hire, but he claims that it is a difficult sell and often a fruitless effort. The need for change in how organizations hire comes as a direct result of the paradigm shift. Be first to adopt this mentality and harvest the talent. Be last to adopt it and lose out on talent.

Drop the checkbox approach to hiring. Checking all the boxes ensures nothing. Try using the trait assessment snapshot tool presented in the first chapter. Assess the head, the heart, and the skills of candidates and let the check marks fall where they may—within reason, of course.

Leading on-the-fly has a great impact on L&D, especially as it relates to the hiring process. The pressure to fill positions in the never-fast-enough workplace has forced the hand of hiring managers to take shortcuts like checking all the boxes rather than checking all the talent. Great hiring leaders will seize the opportunity and convince senior leaders to be talent-focused and not checkbox-focused.

Systems That Work

How work systems are conceived and supported by assets is another extremely important factor in building agile organization structures. Before we get started, I hearken back to the fathers of the business process reengineering movement Michael Hammer and Jim Champy, coauthors of the *New York Times* best seller *Reengineering the Corporation.*

Maestros of change, they broke down the change process into tasks and proved time and again that by reorganizing the tasks—or in the case of IWs, their activities—performance improvement would ensue. IWs perform a series of activities that are organized into work systems. How they are designed and executed is vital to ensure the quality of the collaborative process.

The most generally accepted definition of a work system according to Google is "a system in which human participants and/or machines perform work seen as a process using information, technology, and other resources to produce products or services for internal or external customers." This description sets the stage for understanding the importance in building structures that promote agility in the organizations.

Work that IWs perform doesn't conform to project management principles. Therefore, IW activities are not managed in the classic sense of work systems where a variety of dedicated tools (e.g., PERT charts, workflow management tools, project management software) are used to organize and track progress to completion in a sequential manner.

IWs are left to their own devices to manage their activities and the critical information they need to contribute value. These activities cover a wide spectrum of tasks from generating an invoice to onboarding an employee, getting budget approval to getting an appointment with a customer.

Management experts for years have studied how the missteps on the part of IWs impact performance—and the picture they paint isn't pretty. Clearly, IW activities are part of work systems that in many cases are leftovers from the information age or, worse yet, from the industrial age.

According to most performance experts, including myself, this is a leadership snafu, and until properly addressed, there can be little hope of optimizing the collaborative process through IW participation.

Case in Point: Senior Vice President—Major Retail Bank

This senior leader in a top-tier retail bank was searching for a better way to manage the performance of twenty-five vice presidents. In a discovery session, I asked what his typical week entailed. What he laid out was a hectic four days of traveling between branches debriefing with his vice presidents across the region and then a down day at his office to catch up on paperwork, follow-ups, and generating reports.

In the final analysis, his bank was not equipped with modern work systems or advanced technology necessary to effectively manage the business process. His frustration with the situation was obvious. Like so many other operating leaders, he had accepted it as part of the modern workplace and found himself complaining about it often.

With almost thirty years in banking, he claimed that the systems used to manage the day-to-day work are not much different now than they were several years ago. He further indicated that all banks operate pretty much the same way. When discussing the type of work performed by his VPs, we found much of it to be low value work that was recurring. This was low-hanging fruit that could be automated.

"There must be a better way, and I'd like to find it!" This was the senior vice president's reaction after running a few discovery sessions assessing the organizational structure and the work systems that the bank employed. He sensed that by selecting the right technology and making a few organizational adjustments, he could be up to 50 percent more productive. The initiative, although thwarted by the pandemic, is due to restart.

Work systems are extremely important in retail banking. They are the workhorse of organizational life. Part of the paradigm shift that banks face involves reevaluating the design and support of the business model and enhancing customer service.

The challenge to redesign work systems that better support the structures of a business model must in some way bring agility to the fore. How work systems are organized is usually industry-bound (e.g., healthcare versus consumer goods). The industry often dictates how work systems are designed. Many times, leaders want the best-of-breed work systems seen in an industry.

And sometimes the business environment is so volatile that a company must experiment with multiple work systems to get it right so agile structures can ensue. Complexity in how work is performed is all around us. Leaders who possess agile qualities will be more likely to command the workplace and influence the workforce to get the job done.

Sense and Response

People need their interactions with work systems to be simple, intuitive, and pleasurable so they can productively contribute value to the business process. Connecting the workforce to company goals and sharing outcomes make them more engaged and enlightened as to why their efforts matter.

In the 2017 Deloitte Millennial Survey, they found

Millennials believe a flexible workplace culture supports greater productivity and employee engagement while enhancing personal well-being, health, and happiness. But millennials are not the only employees with high expectations for their places of work. Competition for skilled resources is high, which gives the advantage to the players to negotiate perks that matter to them, such as alternative work arrangements and flexibility.

Today, workers seek companies that consider lifestyle balance to be an important factor in choosing an employer. This trend can be seen in all industries. It influences how work systems are designed to accommodate this new generation of workers.

This is a critical dimension to good leadership, as the workforce is much more diverse today than ever before. It is composed of full-time and part-time workers, contractors who see their stints with companies as short-term gigs, and flip players who serve a purpose on staff until replaced with a permanent employee or are simply no longer needed.

The movement toward the "flex" workforce has many benefits for employees and employers, but it doesn't come without its challenges. Leaders must ensure that these workers are productive and engaged in a common purpose, as their need to balance work and life is out of touch with traditional work system norms.

An ongoing vigilance to revisit work systems is essential. Even work systems that were created only a few years ago may no longer be relevant. And if you are one of those leaders who persists in hanging on to traditional work systems as if they were your favorite pair of slippers, you are missing out on potentially big returns.

Though the word "design" has historically been equated to aesthetics and artistic crafts, this is changing rapidly. Today, taking a design-centric approach to work systems is the mechanism of choice for modern organizations.

In Outcome Dynamics, this approach is called Sense and Response. It helps leaders to design work systems from emotional language rather than from utility. Organizations that get this concept right use emotional language (words that concern desires, aspirations, engagement, and experience) to describe the value in products and services.

> An ongoing vigilance to revisit work systems is essential. Even work systems that were created only a few years ago may no longer be relevant.

Team members discuss the emotional resonance of a value proposition as much as they discuss utility and product requirements. The combination of emotional expression and utility of product application defines the future of work system design, providing a well-rounded perspective of how customers feel and think.

Let's take a closer look. A traditional value proposition is a promise of utility: if you buy an expensive car, the automaker may promise that you will receive safe and comfortable transportation in a well-designed high-performance vehicle. Whereas a design-centric value proposition is a promise of feeling: if you buy an expensive car, the automaker may promise that you will feel pampered, luxurious, and affluent.

In design-centric organizations, emotionally charged language isn't considered silly or frivolous. In fact, focusing on the emotional language has often proved to be a more effective mechanism to respond to the ever-changing customer and competitive conditions quickly.

Take the finance department, for example. Typically, their customers are external to the company and receive contact through invoicing or collections. Traditionally, the work systems supporting them are designed to maximize internal efficiencies. Every time they touch customers, they leave emotional fingerprints. Listening to these impressions and building work systems that react to them is the essence of design-centric work systems.

When conducting Value Dynamics Testing, we are primarily looking for the emotional response versus the utility response. This sensing of the emotional reaction has proved to be a far more effective way to interpret customer reactions. Once tests are scored and interpreted, inferences can be made regarding how to appropriately respond.

Design thinking was first used to make physical objects. Increasingly, it is applied to complex, intangible issues, such as how to shape a customer experience where they emotionally feel more comfortable. Regardless of the context, design thinkers tend to use physical models, also known as design artifacts, to explore, define, and communicate.

These models supplement and sometimes replace the spreadsheets, specifications, and other documents that have come to define the traditional organizational environment. They add a fluid dimension to the exploration of complexity, allowing for nonlinear thought when tackling nonlinear complex problems. This relates to the study by Allen that demonstrates how complexity in decision-making is growing exponentially.

Leaders who only used utility as the benchmark to design work systems are following the fast-growing trend of a design-centric approach to work. For some leaders, emotional language is not measurable, so it's not relevant. Be aware, though, that the design-centric movement is part of the paradigm shift, so it must be seriously considered.

Balancing the Bias

There was a noteworthy study conducted in 2020 by Korn Ferry, a renowned human resources and management consulting firm, titled "Majority of CEOs See More Value in Technology Than Their Workforce." In it, they surveyed eight hundred business leaders in *Fortune* 500 companies to learn that "Leaders may be facing what experts call a 'tangibility bias,' in which, when presented with uncertainty, they are putting priority in their thinking, planning, and execution on the tangible—what they can see, touch and measure, such as technology investments."

As a student of organization life, I find the results of the study alarming, especially coming from Korn Ferry, whose business, of all things, is people. However, the study goes on to defend the position that having a "tangible bias," although common among leaders today, can be dangerous if they lose sight of the fact that technology is only as good as the people that it serves.

To be candid, this mindset needs to be reset. Albeit I am an ardent fan of the role that technology is playing in reshaping the organization of tomorrow, it is not the end-all and be-all to succeed. Indeed, possessing a tangible bias in an unpredictable world is to be expected. Leaders must heed the warning signs of overestimating the value of technology and underestimating the value of the human element in addressing the convergence challenge.

Leaders are caught between a rock and a hard place when it comes to placing their bets. Just be cognizant of the fact that when the pandemic dust settles, people will matter most in the rebuilding. Carefully balancing the bias between technology and people is a critical dimension of good leadership, especially when mapping out a company's forward strategy.

No doubt the pandemic significantly affected how leaders think about their business. Being extremely risk averse is one example. Many leaders have taken a wait-and-see attitude as their industry emerges from the economic rubble that the pandemic has left in its wake. The future of markets and competitor conditions have changed in many industries, but even during the height of the pandemic, great leaders found ways to capitalize on the chaos.

Case in Point: Founder/CEO— Bedding Apparel Manufacturer

In the early stage of the pandemic, the sales of his Midwest company were precipitously plummeting. Being a consummate entrepreneur, the CEO decided to proactively take advantage of manufacturing lines down due to the economic condition. He quickly reacted by making face masks for the public to protect against COVID-19.

The conversion effort was relatively easy because he has been in the business of making cloth products for years. Many other manufacturers soon followed suit, converting unproductive assets into productive assets by making products to address the terrible effects of COVID-19.

This CEO turned chaos into an opportunity, just as Peter Drucker predicted. He went on to appear on several talk shows and at the White House, which further increased his company's exposure. The sales of the company skyrocketed.

His company was agile. It quickly reacted to market and competitive conditions. While serving the greater good, he was able to save the firm. What looked like chaos to others, this CEO turned into opportunity.

In this case, the bedding apparel company quickly turned around their production lines to solve an immediate social need. This is an example of an agile organization that quickly responded to fluid market conditions. This CEO credited his people for the turnround and explained that they were his most coveted asset. His view is not the trending view!

Summary

It can be exhausting for leaders to continue moving the organization forward as the paradigm shift in organizational life unfolds. Although the pandemic caused leaders to be concerned about where they place their bets, just remember that technology is there to serve the greater good of the organization: customers, stakeholders, and shareholders.

In building the collaborative organizations of tomorrow, keep in mind that IWs are a burgeoning segment of the workforce. As a drag on performance, they offer the greatest opportunity to improve performance through collaboration. Part of moving an organization forward requires the creation of more open-border structures that encourage a bottom-up approach so workers can readily participate in the collaborative process and contribute value to results. Structures should be built more like willow trees, not oaks.

Work systems are the workhorse of organizational life. They must be well conceived using a Sense and Response approach to design that includes agility, flexibility, and scalability.

FOCUS FACTOR #3

To *outfocus* competitors, leaders must be moving the organization forward creating structures and work systems that quickly react to fluid market and competitive conditions.

- Leaders must focus on developing agile qualities so they can lead by example, positively command the workplace, and influence the workforce to move forward.

- Leaders must focus on contending with ambiguity and risk, especially in matrix-managed organizations where they may not own the hammer to get the job done.

- Leaders must focus on creating design-centric work systems where emotional language and utility are equally important in delivering value to customers.

CHAPTER 4

EMBRACE THE FUTURE

What and Why of Focus

Leaders are in a collaboration race, and the stakes are high. To compete, leaders must take full advantage of all that advanced technology has to offer. Great leaders want to know *what* to focus on to optimize collaborative processes through automation and *why* obstacles like threatened workforces and the unknowns of technology must not stand in the way.

IN THE LAST CHAPTER, we learned the importance of making the right organizational moves in contending with the convergence challenge, emphasizing that agility, above all other organizational attributes, is key to survival. To make the right moves requires structures and work systems that can quickly react to fluid market and competitor conditions.

In this chapter, we turn our attention to technology. Leaders stand at a crossroads, having to make the decision to add more of the same technology to keep pace with competitors or to adopt next-generation technology to help leapfrog competitors. Either way, you will learn that technology enables the organization to compete on the battlefield of tomorrow.

Our go-to expert on excellence, Tom Peters, wrote in his book, *The Excellence Divided*, "A major part of being committed to excellence is an executive's ability to focus on the many ways that technology can enhance, and in some cases, revolutionize, how we design, conduct, and execute work." Clearly, the leading authority on excellence believes that a commitment to excellence means a commitment to technology.

Let's put another stake in the ground. Technology holds all the cards when it comes to moving the organization closer toward excellence. Everything else is simply window dressing, and great leaders get this. They recognize that unless they push the envelope on the use of technology, their organization may become collaboration age roadkill.

We have established that workplace and workforce dynamics are changing at light speed with the paradigm shift. At the center of it all is the evolution of work. In the age of collaboration, how leaders leverage technology to transform work is a critical aspect of good leadership.

But leaders face a conundrum. The workforce often feels disconnected from the workplace because of technology, and many workers believe that their jobs are in jeopardy due to technology. Some workers even fear that robots are taking over the world, and the idea of having them as digital coworkers is scary at best. But automate we must!

A 2019 Gallop Report concluded, "Fewer than one-third of employees feel engaged with their work, and that half of American jobs are at risk due to technology." To a degree, it is expected that there is a fear of the unknown when it comes to technology. But irrespective of workers' sentiments, leaders must look toward technology to build the collaborative organization of tomorrow.

No longer can human shoulders bear the full brunt of performing all aspects of work. Excellence demands that digital coworkers do their part to free up human hands and augment human intelligence. As you will see in this chapter, the movement toward using robots as coworkers to help humans get the job done is not just smart—it's mandatory.

> Excellence demands that digital coworkers do their part to free up human hands and augment human intelligence.

Michael Porter, our go-to expert on value-based management, wrote the following in his book, *On AI, Analytics, and the New Machine Age*, "Leveraging AI (artificial intelligence) and ML (machine learning) to catapult performance is mandatory to remain competitive, and unless leaders see the future of applying these tools soon, they will never garner their true impact to outperform competitors, as it will be too late."

This is a shot over the proverbial bow! Leaders who wait to embrace the future of technology will be left behind at the station, according to Porter. Those leaders not on board may miss the biggest opportunity of their career. The bookend attributes required for leaders to get aboard are openness and willingness. Without these attributes, failure slaps them in the face.

It doesn't matter whether it's a lion roaring on the hillside seeking advanced technology to gain the competitive advantage or an ostrich with its head in the sand hoping this all goes away. Technology will continue its relentless march forward, changing every aspect of work, and those leaders who are not keeping up will simply have to suffer the competitive consequences.

Automate or Capitulate

We really do live in an exciting time! The tremors reverberating throughout organizations caused by the paradigm shift are to be expected as all facets of work are up for grabs. In the final analysis, the quest to maximize the ROI on human capital demands that leaders leverage technology to the hilt, as it is the surest way to expand human capacity and capabilities in a do-more-with-less business environment.

Technology encompasses a broad spectrum of how information is produced and transferred. To make this work, many convergent and linked technologies are required. The modern information ecosystem is composed of not just computers and devices, but data recognition equipment, communications technology, and complex technology support services.

The mechanisms that enable collaboration to occur are called "facilitated networks." These networks ensure knowledge sharing across the ecosystem of an organization. Leveraging these networks to enhance the collaborative process is extremely important to out-collaborate competitors.

In a 2021 article titled "Innovation Oversight" by Janet Foutty and Bill Brigs from Deloitte, the authors made the following claim: "With the increasing complexity of known and unknown strategic drivers, not only are the strategies becoming more digitally focused, but the use of platforms based on analytics, automation, and AI is digitizing the process of developing and executing strategies and monitoring outcomes."

As complexity in the workplace continues to grow, leaders must look to digitize as much of the business process as possible from goal setting through execution. We learned earlier, leaders have a Cognitive Breakpoint beyond which their ability to lead is greatly diminished or shuts down altogether. Digitalizing as much of the process as possible helps leaders cope. And as Peters suggests, a commitment to excellence means taking full advantage of all that technology has to offer. Now imagine doing this on a single platform, as you'll see in chapter five.

The challenge in contending with the convergence of technology and the human element is best articulated in a 2020 *Forbes* article titled "Moving from the Information Age to the Collaboration Age":

> Humans and machines work seamlessly together. And automation—machine to machine collaboration—will be crucial. Those businesses that get these elements right will boost employee satisfaction and attract the best talent. It sounds good, but how do businesses transition from the Information Age to the Collaboration Age?

This *Forbes* article speaks volumes about the convergence challenge and the role that advanced technology plays. Robots working side by side with humans while also working side by side without humans is the future of work, as the article suggests. The reality is that humans need digital coworkers to lighten the load, boost employee satisfaction, and attract the best talent. The takeaway from this article is to automate or capitulate!

While going through the paradigm shift between ages, workers must come to grips with technology and not see it as the enemy. Herein lies the crux of the tug-of-war between the pull of technology and the pull of human resistance to adapt. The tug-of-war is being experienced across all industries and businesses of every size, affecting industries you might not even expect.

Case in Point: Director— Pharmaceutical Market Research

Since our inception, the research division of our firm has conducted a multitude of studies on organization and leadership. Over the last few years, our firm has conducted extensive field research for a major pharmaceutical research company acting as a subcontractor.

The director of research explained how, prior to the pandemic, researchers joined sales representatives and medical science liaisons (MSLs) in the field, capturing critical data in physician encounters. She further discussed how researchers accompanied the sales representative and MSLs while performing their daily routine, making calls in physician offices and hospitals.

When the coronavirus struck the United States, the president shut down the economy and the research assignment came to a screeching halt. It stayed silent until early fall, when it was resurrected on a limited basis, conducting virtual interviews.

To adjust to the fluid market condition presented by the pandemic, the leadership team of the research firm had to rethink every aspect of the business. This exercise tested the mettle of the organization structures and the work systems that support them. In the end, the firm was able to quickly react to the market and competitive conditions.

Perhaps just as important is the behavior change required on behalf of all parties involved, including researchers, physicians, sales representatives, MSLs, and even corporate data teams who compile results. To their credit, the contractor did an outstanding job crossing the economic chasm created by the pandemic. Their leaders selected the right technology and made the right organization moves to remain competitive.

The jury is still out regarding the long-term use of communication tools to conduct research. But without a doubt, it will not completely die out and may even become the new normal as customers realize the economic efficiencies.

I recently had an interesting interview with the CIO of a very high-end food distribution company. The conversation was about organization and technology and led to a discussion on the effectiveness of conducting virtual meetings to run operations. This CIO shared how difficult it is to manage operations using communication platforms especially when there are many parties involved.

Case in Point: CIO/Officer— Fine Foods Distributor

This executive held many positions in *Fortune* 50 and mid-market companies over her esteemed career. Steeped in technology, marketing, and supply chain knowledge, this executive understands what's at stake in the race to out-collaborate competitors.

In the interview, we discussed how the pandemic put distance management in the spotlight. The CIO emphatically stated, "Communication tools are necessary in that they enable our teams to work visually, but they do nothing to move the needle on improving operational performance between team members, which is desperately needed."

Though there is a plethora of communication platforms to select from, they do nothing to improve how coworkers collaborate around the business process. To be certain, they were a growing part of organizational life long before the pandemic, but now they will be a permanent fixture.

Technically, these platforms are classified as collaboration tools by preeminent research firms like Gartner and IDC Research, who track and assess technology. But in practice, most leaders simply see them as communication tools.

This CIO predicts, "Someday there will be a way to virtually communicate and manage operations while better serving executive needs. I think that this is a problem just waiting for a solution."

During the pandemic, we interviewed several US leaders regarding the use of communication platforms to run a business. Almost to the person, they believe that running virtual sessions, especially when multiple participants are involved, further complicates the workplace and leaves many participants feeling lost and frustrated.

Case in Point: Senior Vice President— Major Technology Security Company

When we interviewed this SVP, he had just got off a virtual call with eighteen internal team members. The meeting agenda centered around development of a sales strategy to reposition its product in the market.

When asked about his experience on the virtual session, his first comment was "It was a mess. Everyone was using different methods to capture notes and exchange information, and there was no way to seamlessly integrate the information into my world."

This is a typical reaction. Even though the session was powered by a well-known communications platform, it only enabled teams to have face time and to record the session so participants could listen later—not a bad thing, but just not enough.

I asked why he could not connect the dots to his world from the meeting by simply reviewing the recording. He admitted, "I think I have reviewed videos from meetings once. Meetings are generally an hour long, and I do not have the time to be running new meetings and reviewing old meeting recordings—it's just unrealistic."

This SVP was one of over fifty leaders interviewed during the pandemic concerning their experience using communication platforms to manage the business process. Almost every leader echoed the frustration this SVP expressed. The evidence is clear: the meteoric rise in using communication platforms will continue, albeit they are not the ultimate answer to managing the business process remotely.

A Tipping Point

The heading of this section is the title of a book authored by Malcolm Gladwell, the legendary social scientist at Yale University. It accurately represents what is occurring in the technology world with the super-growth of cloud solutions.

Here are a few mind-blowing statistics. Gartner released a study approximately four months into the pandemic showing that the global spend on collaboration technology in 2021 is expected to top $100B. Then in 2022, it is expected to double to $200B. These are staggering numbers compared to historical data, and there seems to be no end in sight.

The Gartner study further found that the number one category of technology investment through 2025 will be in the form of SaaS solutions. The spend on SaaS products is exploding before our very eyes. They have become the go-to solution to help leaders manage almost every aspect of operations.

So let's talk cloud! SaaS solutions had been stiff-armed by IT departments for years, mostly due to security issues, but that is all behind us now. Today, IT departments welcome them with open arms. There are many reasons for organizations to adopt cloud solutions. Three of the most widely accepted are they are cost effective, easy to onboard, and easy to expand in new areas of the organization. Hence their appeal.

There are literally hundreds of SaaS solutions available today. Two examples that are very recognizable are Salesforce.com, the leading customer relationship management (CRM), and Workday, a leading human resources and finance software. SaaS solutions puts more power in the hands of the individual worker, which increases workload on the workforce. At the same time, it reduces the company's operating costs. In effect, SaaS solutions are a double-edged sword—they cut both ways!

But SaaS solutions are a tipping point in the application of technology from which there is no turning back. Their growth rate is stupefying. They are affordable, simple-to-learn, and easy-to-use solutions that require no backend support from already overburdened IT departments. And they encourage a bottom-up approach to collaboration.

To further emphasize the connection between SaaS solutions and employee engagement, I refer to an October 2019 Hype-Cycle Report from Gartner that states,

Digital workplace leaders must confirm that their UCC (Unified Communications and Collaboration) strategy addresses the growing importance of worker engagement. Innovations in digital workplace applications continue to emerge, and the cloud has become the standard delivery model changing how UCC is procured, deployed and consumed.

The essential phrase in this report is "growing importance of worker engagement." SaaS solutions encourage worker engagement, which contributes to the collaborative process. Another attraction is their delivery model. Offered on a subscription basis, the company provides the maintenance, support, and upgrades as part of the subscription agreement. The trend toward SaaS solutions is undeniable, as advantages such as these are hard for leaders to resist.

The decision to use a SaaS solution usually resides with the operating leader who wants to use it. This is a dramatic change from the previous era where IT departments controlled all technology. No longer! Operating leaders can try before they buy and then sign up to use a SaaS independent of IT departments getting involved.

Leaders' time is precious. They can ill afford to go through lengthy approval processes. All they need to do is get the IT department to ensure that the SaaS meets the company's security policies, and they can be off and running.

Very Scary Things

Across disciplines, researchers are hard at work studying the implications that automation has on the workplace in general and specifically on the human element. The appetite on the part of leaders to automate is ferocious, and the need to do so gets more compelling as the hands of time pass. But sensitivity to the human element to adopt advanced technology must be factored into the decision as well. Good leadership requires it.

Many workers view robots as very scary things. Just mentioning the word sends chills up and down their spines. They imagine something out of a sci-fi movie where robots take over the earth. Putting the sentiments of workers aside, the use of robots will continue to explode over the decades to come regardless of how workers feel.

Robots (nicknamed "bots") provide a threefold advantage to organizational performance: they eliminate human error, reduce operating cost, and expand human capacity and capabilities. This combination is a hard proposition for leaders to ignore.

Automating work dramatically improves the ROI on human capital, which in a do-more-with-less world is exactly what the business performance doctor (that would be me) prescribes.

Case in Point: VP Customer Service—Retail Banking

This senior leader was responsible for customer support across a region of a large bank. In a discover session, she shared how technology is used to manage customer support issues, stating, "The bank's goal is to achieve a level of competency where 90 percent of customer support issues can be handled with no human involvement." The bank, she said, had not quite reached that goal but was gaining on it.

She and I discussed at some length the tug-of-war between man and machine. Jokingly, I alluded to the number of times that I was on a call addressing a banking issue with a customer support robot when it got into a tailspin and I got caught up in a vicious loop. Speaking to a live person is, of course, the option of last resort. Who hasn't found themselves so frustrated that they end up yelling at the phone, "Give me a live person!"

The point is, in the past this happened often, and today it occurs less frequently. The reason? Robots learn and correct. That's what they do. She agreed that it is not a frequent occurrence anymore but commented, "I can't tell you how often we get calls from customers complaining about having to communicate through technology at all. My staff is constantly reminding customers that if everyone waited for a live person to address their banking needs, they would be on hold forever."

Neither this bank nor any other bank is about to give up robots handling customer service issues, as this is now the accepted practice to compete. The economics of reverting to the old days would be disastrous. Robots eliminate low-skill work, eliminate human error, reduce operating expense, and expand human capacity and capabilities to perform more value-rich work.

The movement toward the use of robots may not agree with everyone, but it is unstoppable. Visualize for a moment the work your organization performs today that will be automated over the next decade. Now imagine the work that you could not envision that will also be automated. Truly, we live in exciting times!

> The movement toward the use of robots may not agree with everyone, but it is unstoppable.

To those who feel that robots are very scary things, understand that they are not new to business. They have been performing work in industries for decades in backroom operations and on manufacturing floors. What is remarkable about robots today is how quickly they are gaining ground in the life of IWs, a segment of the workforce that is tripling every year.

AI-Automation Movement

The use of AI has been investigated for more than sixty years. Since inception, development of computing power has exponentially grown, innovative algorithms of application have developed, and the gathering of massive data has been made possible.

As technology continues to transform the nature of work, how the human element factors into the equation is rapidly changing. The purpose of advanced technology is to eliminate burdensome tasks and improve the lives of workers. Technology is meant to increase human productivity and provide humans a chance to concentrate on more enjoyable, value-rich work that they were hired to do.

We have always seen adjustments in the workplace and workforce when new technologies become available. But the speed at which advance technologies are changing organization dynamics has a direct impact on leadership. Awe-inspiring as it is, leaders across all industries are grappling with the challenge to keep pace.

As an outgrowth of the preponderant use of advanced technology, we have come to the point where AI-enabled automation, seen as a combination of Robotic Process Automation (RPA) and artificial intelligence (AI) technologies, rules the roost. Together, they empower rapid end-to-end business process automation and accelerate digital transformation.

This has been the case for some time with blue-collar work. The manufacturing floor of most companies looks more like a robotics convention. The only humans in sight are those needed to oversee operations, not to perform the work. As automation changed the nature of work in manufacturing, it is changing the nature of work in the office.

In the not too distant future, AI will infiltrate every corner of organizational life. Hardware and software bots will run many aspects of the operation. Today, the heavy lifting is done by three technologies: AI, ML, and RPA. However, there are a couple of technologies whose stars are precipitously rising. Though they are in their infancy, they may hold the greatest potential for changing how work is designed, conducted, and executed.

The first is blockchain. This advanced technology takes the friction out of business operations. It is especially effective in high-volume transaction businesses. Unlike any of the other technologies, it works by leveraging multiple computers linked in a peer-to-peer network that simultaneously creates, maintains, and tracks transactions.

The concept may be a bit difficult to wrap your head around, but just know that it provides a dimension of speed, accuracy, and account-ability to transacting business securely. Our go-to innovation expert, Clayton Christiansen, would consider this to be "disruptive innova-tion." Leaders aware of this technology often associate it with bitcoin or cryptocurrency, where it was first introduced, but that is changing fast.

Blockchain may offer the greatest long-term potential to build the collaborative organization of tomorrow. Of all the technologies mentioned, blockchain is in its embryotic stage of development.

As I write, there are many new uses for blockchain being explored beyond currency exchange. It could be the grandaddy of all technolo-gies when it comes to changing workplace and workforce dynamics. It brings efficiencies in operations the likes of which have never been experienced.

Envision a world in which contracts are embedded in digital code and stored in transparent, shared databases, where they are protected from deletion, tampering, and revision. In this world, every agreement, every process, every task, and every payment would have a digital record and signature that could be identified, validated, stored, and shared. This is collaboration on steroids.

Intermediaries like lawyers, brokers, and bankers might no longer be necessary. Individuals, organizations, machines, and algorithms would freely transact and interact with one another with no boundaries to cross. Information would flow freely—almost effortlessly—across the ecosystem of the organization, as knowledge would be instantly democratized to those who need it, when they need it.

Another fast-rising star is chatbot technology. This is voice recognition found in mobile devices like Android and iPhone, as well as Alexa. Voice-activated technology has been available for quite some time. Predominantly it has been used to perform simple personal tasks like turning on the lights, turning down the thermometer, and playing music. Recently, a few basic business commands have been added, such as note-taking or setting calendars.

Jeff Bezos, founder of Amazon, claimed that Amazon Web Services (AWS) is betting heavily on Alexa chatbot technology to drive the future of work. His vision is that voice-activation devices like Alexa will someday replace the need for humans to touch a keyboard to manage the business. To date, his vision has been unmet, but he relentlessly pursued it until his resignation in July 2021.

In chapter five, you will be exposed to a next-generation platform that enables leaders and teams to manage business performance on any hands-free device through chatbot technology. Leveraging AI-enabled automation to the max, Bezos's vision has finally been met, as you shall see.

The paradigm shift is occurring at light speed. The AI-enabled automation movement plays a significant role in spurring on workplace and workforce changes as part of the shift. As leaders joust for position to remain on the forefront of the collaboration race, their weapon of choice is automation.

AI GOLD RUSH

How familiar are you with the term "hybrid workforce?" If the answer is not at all or not a lot, then you are in the majority. But it is a term that leaders should quickly get familiar with. Building the collaborative organization of tomorrow requires the workforce to be a hybrid of humans, robots, and systems working in concert to drive results. Hence the term hybrid workforce.

To those leaders who have already embraced this concept, congratulations! You are in the minority. You give workers the opportunity to take on more complex and fulfilling tasks, use creative problem-solving, empathy, negotiation, and acquire more advanced skills. Leaders who do this place themselves in the competitive catbird seat, gaining a leg up on becoming a great leader.

McKinsey recently reported that by 2025, at least one-third of our day-to-day work could be automated in approximately 60 percent of roles. And Gartner estimates that by 2024, 69 percent of routine work will be automated. These statistics leave little doubt that leaders must get on board and adopt the hybrid workforce concept now, before the train leaves the station and it's too late to catch up, as Michael Porter warns.

How do leaders prepare themselves to lead the hybrid workforce? The simple answer is that there are no hard-and-fast rules. To my knowledge, no pages exist in any leadership playbook to explain it. I refer to this period in the AI movement as the "AI gold rush." Akin to the California gold rush, the first in are writing all the rules and reaping all the rewards.

There is no better way to convey the enormity of the AI gold rush than to cite two of the largest robot builders in the world: UI Path and Automation Anywhere. Both publicly traded companies, they started operations a year apart in the early 2000s. Interestingly, both firms struggled for years. Then, as if a light went on, things changed quickly. Leaders by the droves turned to robots to automate work so their organizations could do more with less.

Here is a startling statistic. Between 2019 and 2020, the aggregate common stock value of these two companies rose by $2 billion, and their sole business is building robots. Although UI Path is the larger of the two, Gartner declares Automation Anywhere to be more innovative through their Magic Quadrants (proprietary qualitative data analysis methods to demonstrate market trends, such as direction, maturity, and participants).

Another highly regarded research firm that tracks and assesses the technology industry is IDC Research. They reported that worldwide AI spending will reach $97.9 billion in 2023. This is a significant increase over their original estimate of $77.6 billion. We clearly are on an automation journey that even George Orwell would marvel at.

It staggers the imagination to think what the workplace will be like at the end of this decade. As the AI-enabled automation movement continues to gobble up more and more of the workload that humans perform, the feeding frenzy to automate is intense.

To put the automation journey into perspective, below is UI Path's Enterprise Automation Journey graphic. It depicts the various phases of automation that we are in and will be going through.

ENTERPRISE AUTOMATION JOURNEY

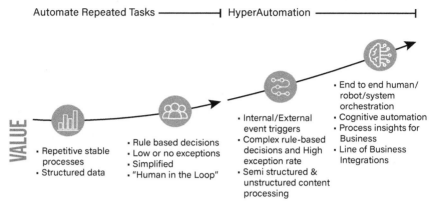

Automate Repeated Tasks ——————| HyperAutomation ——————————|

VALUE

- Repetitive stable processes
- Structured data

- Rule based decisions
- Low or no exceptions
- Simplified
- "Human in the Loop"

- Internal/External event triggers
- Complex rule-based decisions and High exception rate
- Semi structured & unstructured content processing

- End to end human/robot/system orchestration
- Cognitive automation
- Process insights for Business
- Line of Business Integrations

TIME

Everything on the left side of the curve has been accomplished and is being applied in many companies today. Recently, we have seen much progress under the blue side of the curve. Bots performing repetitive low-value work with no human involvement is a booming trend and is an inevitable part of the organization of tomorrow.

At the same time, we are headed for the high ground of what advanced technology has to offer. Here, cognitive automation kicks in to augment human intelligence. It will bring with it insight into operations, integrating business lines and revolutionizing decision-making. This is where advanced technology pays big dividends.

But I do not want to mislead. While the primary driver of the hybrid workforce is to augment how humans perform work and expand human intelligence, low-skill jobs may be at risk. As in the case of the customer service VP in the retail bank example, their goal is to have robots handle 90 percent of the customer support issues with no human involvement.

This effort has and will continue to impact jobs. More than likely, the bank will see low-skill jobs in customer service and other areas go by the wayside, being replaced by more high-skilled jobs that may not even exist today.

The interconnectivity of technologies has long lagged behind market demand. This, too, is changing. We will see a host of partnerships and marriages between companies that will propel collaboration to unimaginable heights. Add to this the advances made in application program interfaces (APIs) that facilitate the integration of the on-site and off-site workforce, and one can see why we are on an unequaled automation journey.

There may be no better example of a marriage between companies than the recent partnership between Verizon and Amazon's AWS to offer 5G capability. This opens a new realm of possibilities for collaboration, as 5G technology imparts more speed in communications and improves the streaming of information, both of which are core to optimizing the collaborative process.

Another good example of a marriage between companies in the SaaS space was the 2021 acquisition of Slack by Salesforce.com. Slack is a collaboration hub that brings the right people, information, and tools together to get work done. The purchase expands Salesforce capacity and capability to connect users of Salesforce.com to the world.

Keeping Salesforce.com in the limelight, another example is their acquisition of a California start-up company called Griddible in 2019. This Silicon Valley firm provides technology that synchronizes data in the cloud, expanding the user's capability to access, store, and retrieve customer data and providing users with an extended seamless customer experience.

Advanced technology enables the organization to facilitate connectivity throughout the ecosystem, boosting productivity, creativity, and innovation to outperform competitors. Uninterrupted wireless access to share and retrieve information propels the collaborative process.

So where is this all headed? Futurists for decades have espoused the notion of the "anywhere, anytime workforce" concept. This is the ultimate objective. To participate, leaders must be open and willing to embrace the hybrid workforce concept where humans, robots, and systems work in concert to produce results. To accomplish this is the mark of a great leader in the twenty-first century.

> Leaders must be open and willing to embrace the hybrid workforce concept where humans, robots, and systems work in concert to produce results.

Summary

We are experiencing the greatest period of technological advances ever witnessed. Driven by AI-enabled automation, collaboration has been catapulted to the top of the leadership discussion. I call this time in the movement the AI gold rush, where the first in are writing all the rules and reaping all the rewards.

The movement is driven by several technologies: artificial intelligence, ML, RPA, blockchain, and chatbot. The movement will eventually touch every aspect of organizational life, expanding the human capacity and capability to do more with less—improving the ROI on human capital.

Robots are our digital coworkers. They enable humans to perform more value-rich work and to augment human intelligence in decision-making. And as we augment human intelligence and digitalize the business process from strategy through execution, collaboration will take on a whole new meaning.

FOCUS FACTOR #4

To *outfocus* competitors, leaders must be leveraging advance technology to expand the capacity and capability of humans to perform work and optimize the ROI on human capital.

- Leaders must focus on adopting the hybrid workforce concept to ensure that their organization remains on the forefront of the collaborative movement.

- Leaders must focus on digitizing strategies and monitoring outcomes to improve how work is performed and make it a high strategic priority.

- Leaders must focus on the many ways that advanced technology can optimize the collaborative process critical to compete on the battlefield of tomorrow.

CHAPTER 5

GO THE EXTRA MILE

What and Why of Focus

Leaders are frustrated and disoriented using fragmented resources to manage the business process. Leaders realize that they are woefully inadequate and stand in the way of optimizing collaboration. Great leaders want to know *what* to focus on to hyper-collaborate and *why* obstacles like resistance to change and dealing with the unknown of advanced technology must not stand in the way.

WELCOME TO THE MUCH-ANTICIPATED fifth chapter. Not meant for the faint of heart, this chapter is for progressive leaders looking to go the extra mile and ensure that they can out-collaborate competitors and *outfocus* competitors to gain the competitive advantage.

To accomplish this objective, leaders are introduced to a one-of-a kind approach that optimizes the collaborative process. Included in the approach is an AI-driven performance platform that even Clayton Christensen, our go-to innovation expert, would consider to be disruptive innovation. But before getting started, let's recap what we have learned thus far about the convergence challenge.

From a leadership perspective, there exists an insidious workplace phenomenon dubbed on-the-fly leadership. We discussed how it produces a fallout on the Core Leadership Functions and a blowback effect on the ability of leaders to volitionally focus their attention referred to as Attention Deficit Syndrome.

From an organizational perspective, we learned what it takes to build an agile organization that can quickly react to fluid market and competitive conditions. This includes moving toward open-border structures with work systems that are flexible and scalable and encourage bottom-up participation. Emphasis on building a change-ready culture is crucial to preparing the human element for the bombardment of changes occurring in the workplace as the paradigm shift continues to unfold.

From a technology perspective, we learned how an array of advanced technologies make up the AI-enabled automation movement, referring to this time in the movement as the AI gold rush. We further learned that we are on an automation journey that spawns digital coworkers necessary to expand human capacity and capabilities, improving the ROI on human capital. And we learned that as we enter the hyper-automation phase of the journey, advanced technology will not only free up human hands, but augment human intelligence.

Clearly, leaders stand at the crossroads! They must decide whether to remain loyal to the fragmented resource of yesteryear or to adopt a new generation platform that consolidates, integrates, and automates work on a single platform. And don't forget that openness and willing-ness on the part of leaders is required to be successful. For those who want to move forward, let's test your mettle.

Warriors of Progress

Surely, we live in an exciting time! As in the Industrial Revolution, we are in a tug-of-war between man and machine. The vexing questions facing leaders is whether to address the challenge using conventional tools or move on to a next-generation solution. The most telling indicator of a leader's openness and willingness to progress forward is where they stand on the Morse Adoption Life Cycle.

For leaders who are not familiar with the Morse Life Cycle (commonly called the Morse Curve), Morse spent years researching how markets react to technology and what types of users adopt them first and last. The curve has withstood the test of time for decades and remains the bellwether mechanism to understand market dynamics surrounding technology.

Below is the Morse Curve. Take a moment. Test yourself. See where you fit on the curve. Know that the farther left on the curve you are, the more likely it is that you will adopt an innovative solution.

The farther right on the curve you are, the more likely it is that you will stay with the "tried 'n' true."

When placing yourself on the curve, be honest! This exercise is meant to save you the trouble of reading on if you are not a good candidate for adopting a first-generation solution. If you want to read on just to be enlightened, be my guest. Be mindful, though, that every successful technology eventually reaches across all categories on the curve. Even laggards, who represent about 10 percent of a market, will eventually adopt next-generation technology.

Confidence is a gift, and, used wisely, it can open the door to opportunity. Adopting a first-generation platform that changes how leaders and teams collaborate requires confidence on the part of leaders; otherwise it should not be attempted at all.

> Confidence is a gift, and, used wisely, it can open the door to opportunity.

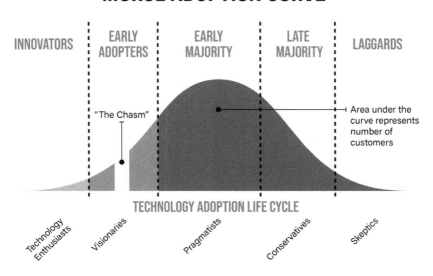

MORSE ADOPTION CURVE

141

Statistically, leaders who initially adopt a first-generation solution will be considered innovators and early adopters. These two categories combined comprise approximately 15 percent of the market. They are the warriors of progress. They see the AI gold rush as their ticket to move the organization closer toward excellence to gain speed on becoming a great leader.

Placing yourself on the curve is the litmus test. If you think you are ready, then read on. It was Henry Ford who said, "Whether you think you can, or you think you can't, you're right!" The same applies to adopting this platform. If you think you can, you're right!

Make Work Smart

Leaders feel frustrated and disoriented. This is not conjecture; it's fact borne out of our study "What Makes Leaders Tick." Out of several options, leaders overwhelmingly selected these two answers to best represent how they feel when struggling to manage organizational performance using multiple disconnected resources. One COO of a midsize healthcare company remarked, "There must be a better way!"

There are many reasons why collaborating with fragmented resources doesn't work well. The three that spurred us on were obvious:

1. A lack of integration in the information residing in the myriad of workflow tools, third-party apps, and internal documents to run the business.

2. There is no single system on a platform that the organization can use to manage all aspects of the day-to-day business process.

3. In managing the business process, as work is performed there is no way to automatically capture and convert critical performance data into intelligence.

After watching the collaboration calamity build over the years, we decided to take matters into our own hands. Our aim was to innovate a new-generation platform that would enable organizations to not just collaborate, but hyper-collaborate. And there is a vast difference between collaboration and hyper-collaboration, as you will learn.

In the previous chapter, we extolled the virtues of advanced technology suggesting that AI-enabled automation holds all the cards to optimize collaboration. We explained why new technologies on the horizon will magnify the scope and pace of change in how we collaborate. We also discussed why leaders who do not take full advantage of technology to collaborate will suffer the competitive consequences.

And we pointed out that many leaders often do not get the full benefit that technology has to offer, as it's used in isolation. Just think of the scores of tabs that are open across the top of your computer screen when performing your portion of the business management process.

Now consider that, for the most part, the data found in the apps behind the tabs are not interconnected, nor are they connected to the day-to-day business process used to run operations. Hence, each works in isolation.

Case in Point: Vice President Operations—*Fortune* 100 Technology Company

This young leader was taken aback by her inability to connect the critical information found on Salesforce.com to the internal planning process of the company: "The only option I was given by the IT department was to have an outside consulting firm build a custom

ERP (enterprise resource package) solution." This, she declared, was a costly, time-consuming effort.

The inability to easily connect the dots between information sources flabbergasted her. She further stated, "Everyone on my team has to go to different places to patch together the information. This is a source of great disturbance, as my teams need to see the big picture on the spot and cannot wait until reports are generated days or weeks later."

The type of information and the timing in which it's needed is the cry of leaders today. Leaders instinctively know that using disconnected resources to capture, analyze, and share information wastes valuable time and resources and kills team productivity.

Upon deciding to take matters into our own hands, we began the innovation process by asking ourselves, "What is the job to be done?" The answer was to create a first-generation AI-driven Performance Automation Platform that makes work smart while simplifying workplace complexity. Our view of the world: don't just work—make work smart!

We made three observations from our research and consulting experience concerning collaboration before getting started:

1. The collaborative process today requires multiple activities and many resources. This opens the door for disconnects, bottlenecks, and voids to bog down the process of producing results, which can end in poor organizational performance. Eliminating work steps by consolidating and integrating resources is an absolute necessity. In essence, the simpler the platform, the better. Do this right to make work smart.

2. The need to automate as much of the repeatable mundane work that IWs perform as possible is inescapable. Humans are able to concentrate on more value-rich work when advanced technology is used to automate low-value work.

This is imperative to optimize the collaborative process. Do this right to make work smart.

3. Moving from automation to hyper-automation, human intelligence will be augmented to help leaders address complexity in decision-making and reporting. This is where advanced technology flexes its muscle and serves the greater good to help leaders outperform competitors. Do this right to make work smart.

These observations stabilize the innovation process. As always, the What and Why of Focus was used throughout the process to keep us on track and to watch our back. With a mission to make work smart by leveraging advanced technology, a breakthrough in how the organization collaborates was within our grasp.

Anywhere, Anytime Workforce

In the effort to create a platform extraordinaire, we discovered that there is more to optimizing the collaborative process than just applying an intelligent platform designed to help the organization achieve hyper-collaboration. But without it, attaining hyper-collaboration is out of the question.

Two other dimensions were considered: the work environment and the work logic. As consultants, we found these to be important factors to optimize the collaborative process. In fact, how leaders meld together these dimensions is indicative of how well the organization collaborates.

Below is a diagram of the three dimensions working in unison. Notice at the center of the diagram is workplace singularity. This is the mecca of organizational success, defined as "a state in which leaders and teams think as one, act as one, and work as one in the process of producing results." To achieve singularity, all three dimensions must work symbiotically.

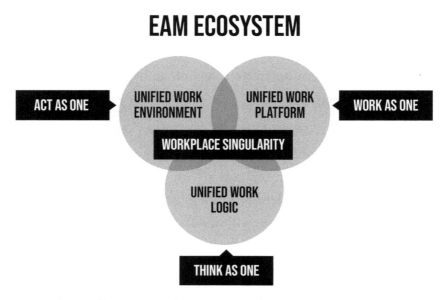

EAM ECOSYSTEM

Like excellence, singularity is viewed as an ongoing pursuit—not a destination. Singularity is something that leaders aspire to while commanding the workplace and influencing the workforce. To be clear, singularity is not a replacement for excellence, but a descriptor of what is occurring in the workplace as leaders move the organization toward excellence. Let's take a brief look at each dimension.

UNIFIED WORK ENVIRONMENT

This first dimension sets the stage for how easy or difficult it is for workers from the C-suite to line managers to collaborate in driving business results. If the workplace environment is not properly prepared to accept the rash of changes accompanying the paradigm shift, then building the collaborative organization of tomorrow will be next to impossible.

As an organizational expert, I enter some companies where the work environment energizes me and lifts my spirit to help resolve a performance challenge. On the flip side, I have entered organizations where the environment drains my energy, and I question whether I can truly help to right the ship.

Granted, our consulting firm is like the fire department of performance. A performance fire has been burning for some time and the work environment has been impacted—that's expected. But using my "sixth sense," I can distinguish between a temporary decline in the work environment due to a business performance challenge and a systemic problem that cuts to the quick of the organization's persona.

One of my favorite management professors in graduate school gave a lecture on how organizations are living, breathing entities where people, structures, and systems come together to create value for customers. I found this description to be simple yet profound. After the lecture, we discussed the implications of his perspective ad nauseum, and I have embraced it ever since.

In fact, chapter three was dedicated to understanding the importance of fine-tuning the dynamics between people, structure, and work systems to produce results. These are the underpinnings upon which optimizing collaboration depends.

We further explored why building an adaptive culture with a change-ready mentality to prepare the human element for the deluge of changes occurring in the workplace is a sign of good leadership. I shared that there are environments that energize me and environments that rob me of energy. The difference between the two usually comes down to culture, specifically these two aspects of culture. They are important. Without cultivating a culture that possesses these characteristics, leaders will find themselves waging an uphill battle as the paradigm shift evolves.

You're the leader. Be proactive. If necessary, drop the command card once again. Educate the workforce on the importance of having a change-ready culture. Instill in them a feeling of confidence, letting them know that when change comes, they will be prepared.

Almost nobody likes change. This is a statistical fact. But you should not have to fight with teams when it is time to change. All traditional norms of organizational life are under fire, and the ability of leaders and teams to quickly react to market and competitive conditions is paramount. This is how leaders and teams *act as one.*

UNIFIED WORK LOGIC

Work logic is the second dimension. It sets the stage for how the organization manages the day-to-day business process at ground level. The need for a single approach from goal setting through execution seems obvious on its face. Some leaders believe that it already exists in their organization while most leaders have shared that it is almost nonexistent.

> Educate the workforce on the importance of having a change-ready culture. Instill in them a feeling of confidence, letting them know that when change comes, they will be prepared.

Early in the book, we discussed the widening gap between planning and execution, citing the works of a few leading research firms. Their studies emphasized how poor performance is on the rise and that the cost on the bottom line of *Fortune* 500 companies alone is staggering. They further claim that it is mostly due to poor execution, especially on the part of IWs.

Fact is, over 80 percent of our clients were experiencing the side effects of the execution gap, many in spades. We also found that the greater the workload on teams, the wider the gap. And as we all know, if left unchecked, work overload alone can lead to chaos in the workplace, which magnifies the effects of the gap.

Getting everyone from the C-suite to line managers on the same page and keeping them there from planning through execution is not a simple nor straightforward task. It requires a business logic that is repeatable and scalable with a common point of view and a common language that coworkers can effectively use to collaborate.

Plan for Planning

To standardize planning through execution, we divide the process into five distinct steps: goal groups, goals, strategies, initiatives, and action items. This five-step process ensures that plans are well thought out, easily communicated, and logically connected throughout the process of producing results.

Segmenting the system into these steps greatly enhances the collaborative process. Applied properly, it will get and keep everyone on the same page. Let's take a brief look at each step.

STEP #1: GOAL GROUPS

Realize that creating goal groups is unique to this process. Dividing the business operations into groups first helps leaders succinctly determine how they will manage their segment of the business.

Goal groups are qualifiable and not quantified. They carry no measurable values. They are simply a way to distinguish how leaders decide to manage the business process. How leaders determine groups is purely dependent on how they view the business. So there is no right or wrong approach.

Creating goal groups is usually influenced by the industry or business segment in which the organization competes. For example, a senior leader like a CEO in a manufacturing company using silo structures to run operations may set up their goal groups by functions (e.g., human resources, finance, sales, marketing).

As pointed out in a previous chapter, silo structures do not encourage worker participation, making it more difficult to optimize the collaborative process. Today, this is more likely to occur in large legacy companies where managing the business process through matrixes is commonplace.

More modern organizations favor open-border structures. In these companies, goal groups could include growth, costs, customers, vendors, and culture. These structures encourage worker participation and help to optimize the collaborative process. This approach also enables cross-functional initiatives to be more easily addressed by encouraging cooperation of team members.

Regardless of how leaders create goal groups to represent the business, create them they must. The rewards to beginning the planning process in this manner will become obvious through application. The risk to doing so is de minimis. Leaders who embrace this approach exhibit another sign of good leadership.

For the remainder of the steps, let's use the goal group revenue as the example.

STEP #2—GOAL SETTING

The relationship between creating goal groups and goal setting is iterative, meaning that not all goal groups need to be identified and locked into place before the goals required to support them are identified. As leaders work among themselves to create a go-forward road map, goals for each group should be discussed concurrently.

Unlike goal groups, goals are qualifiable and quantifiable. I'm utterly amazed how many leaders do not understand that goals must be quantifiable—otherwise they are simply strategies. This is a hard and fast rule in the Plan for Planning process. Goals must be quantifiable—measurable!

At its core, goal setting is a matter of determining the current state of a business and deciding what needs to be accomplished to create a future state. Without goals, leaders would be unable to communicate the direction of an organization or articulate where it stands at any given time along the process, be it for a month, quarter, or fiscal year.

Examples of goal setting for the revenue goal group could be one of these:

1. Improve sales by 3 percent.

2. Increase client base by 5 percent.

3. Acquire twelve new corporate accounts.

Note that each goal is measurable in some way.

STEP #3—STRATEGY

Strategies act as the overarching road map for how an organization is going to achieve a goal. In most cases, more than one strategy is required to attain a goal. Strategies work synergistically to move the organization forward toward accomplishing a goal. Strategies are only qualifiable, not quantifiable!

A strategy is a plan of action. It's not the actual action itself. To my amazement, I've witnessed countless situations in which the term "strategy" was used by leaders to describe an action they were planning on taking. This is not how it is used in this Plan for Planning process.

An example of how to achieve the goal of "acquire twelve new corporate accounts" might be one of the following:

1. Conduct a cold calling campaign.

2. Engage an SEO firm.

3. Hire a corporate engagement officer.

Even though all of these strategies are independent of each other, they work in concert to achieve the same goal: acquire twelve new corporate accounts.

STEP #4—INITIATIVE

If strategies are the overarching road map to achieve a goal, then initiatives are the plan of attack at ground level. Initiatives are where the rubber meets the road. They are like the traffic cops for action items and decide which action items are needed, what they should do, and then coordinate their movement.

An example of three initiatives for the strategy "engage an SEO firm" might be one of these:

1. Create a short list of firms.

2. Phone interview the short list.

3. Conduct a three-firm bake-off.

Note that these initiatives sequentially occur, meaning that they may have come from the same strategy session.

However, they just as easily could have been random, unrelated initiatives:

1. Create a short list of vendors.

2. Have legal prepare agreement.

3. Get funding approval.

These are nonsequential initiatives, but each still moves the ball forward toward the goal of acquiring twelve new corporate accounts.

STEP #5—ACTION ITEM

This is where work takes place and the gap between planning and execution often breaks down. Action items are something that everyone in an organization performs, from the C-suite to the general workforce, and without which there would be no achieving goals.

Many people refer to action items as their to-do list. In our world, we view them as action items since action is required to complete them. Action items always support initiatives, and it's rare to see them connected directly to a strategy.

Examples of three action items in the case of the initiative "get funding approval":

1. Prepare the request.

2. Meet with funding committee.

3. Meet with sales VP to get support.

Action items are constantly added, deleted, and adjusted as an initiative takes form and alters the number and type of action items required to complete the initiative. This is how leaders and teams *think as one.*

Plan for Planning Summary

Providing the workforce with a consistent framework to connect the dots from goal setting through execution is tantamount to possessing a road map to success. As highlighted in the studies conducted by leading research firms early on in this book, planning is not the culprit for poor performance—execution is. Unless planning through execution is seamlessly linked, optimizing the collaborative process will remain out of reach.

UNIFIED WORK PLATFORM

This third dimension brings hyper-collaboration to life. Without a dedicated platform purposed to get the job done, hyper-collaboration is not possible. I'm always astonished when I see leaders acquire more of the same technology, assuming it will improve organizational performance, but it usually ends up being just another Band-Aid.

Frankly, I cannot remember a leader who praised how effective their teams collaborate. Quite the opposite. The mere fact that leaders work so hard to control the direction of organizational performance is very telling about the quality of collaboration, and of course the primary offender is the use of fragmented resources to manage the business process.

When I asked a senior leader in a *Fortune* 100 consumer products company about the quality of collaboration among his teams, he replied, "It is not a good situation, but what is the alternative? We have all the latest and greatest technology, so that is not the answer. I don't know what our competition does, but I assume they feel the same way."

Keep in mind that your competitors are using the same tools and techniques to collaborate as you are. They face the same challenges involved in trying to effectively collaborate while running operations. I often remind leaders when they complain about their plight that the cows grazing on the other side of the fence get indigestion too.

Competitors in the same industries, for the most part, think the same, act the same, and work the same. This is because they use the same resources to collaborate and run the business. And don't think that outworking competitors is an option to outperform them. The McKinsey study made it clear that leaders manage through "immediacy" and cannot get to everything on their plates. Our research not only corroborates this reality, but it further concludes that leaders are already at their limit to cognitively cope with workplace complexity and work overload, as was explained in chapter two.

Let's put another stake in the ground. To outperform competitors, leaders must first *outfocus* them. The aim is to see what competitors can't. If information in the organization is captured, analyzed, and shared when it is needed and in a form that it is needed, then leaders will see things in their business that competitors can't see in their own businesses. This is how to gain the competitive advantage.

Be it in business, sports, or any of life's endeavors, finding ways to gain the advantage defines competition. As I write, the 2020 Olympics are wrapping up in Japan. Throughout the event, sportscasters were constantly talking about the little things that athletes do or need to do to gain the competitive advantage. The burning desire to find an advantage is what drives athletes and business leaders to greatness.

> To outperform competitors, leaders must first *outfocus* them.

And this desire is what spurred the invention of Targa, a first-generation Performance Automation Platform that enables leaders to collaborate on a scale that previously was unimaginable. Crucial to its success is leveraging the hybrid workforce concept where humans, robots, and systems work in concert on a single platform to manage the day-to-day business process.

Just imagine a single AI-driven platform where leaders and teams can seamlessly integrate the following functions: strategic management, task management, chatbot/messenger management, meeting management, RPA, and video conferencing. Add to this list a host of custom-built robots that automate much of the collaborative process. Each of these functions represent a category in the Magic Quadrants—this is hyper-collaboration.

This book is not the appropriate forum to get into the details of how the entire platform works; however, it can provide an overview of the major functions, as you'll see below. For more detailed information, leaders can visit our website (targatek.com) and take Targa for a spin to experience the power or request a demo.

A fifty-thousand-foot tour of the platform is worthwhile. Five distinct yet interconnected segments work in tandem to drive the collaborative process, maximize performance, and move the organization closer toward excellence. Let's take a brief look at each segment and see how each helps to accomplish this end.

1. **Auto-Sync the Process:** Using the five-step Plan for Planning approach to center the collaborative process—goal groups, goals, strategies, initiatives, and action items—the platform automatically synchronizes all the activities involved in each step. This keeps workers on the same page from planning through execution using a common process with a common language. This is how to make work smart!

2. **Integrate Resources:** Critical resources (e.g., workflow tools like One Note, Google Sheets, Smartsheet, and critical third-party apps) to run the operations like Salesforce.com, Workday, or Trillo are consolidated on the platform. Information residing in them can be integrated into the Plan for Planning process and to each other. This is how to make work smart!

3. **Automate Work:** Custom action robots on the platform work alongside humans and work between themselves to enable the organization to do more with less. A simple example of this would be the automation of meetings. The platform's meeting robot sets agendas, coordinates calendars,

takes notes, captures action items, and sends alerts to workers assigned to them with no human involvement. This is how to make work smart!

4. **Predict the Future:** As work is being performed on the platform by humans or robots, performance data is automatically collected in the background. A platform-specific analytics robot analyzes the data and predicts future performance. With a 95 percent accuracy rate, this helps leaders to manage the direction of performance and to quickly react to fluid market and competitive conditions. This is how to make work smart!

5. **Manage Hands-Free:** In the future, managing the business through voice-activated technology is a fait accompli. Hubbi is the first performance command chatbot of its kind to accomplish this objective. Available on any mobile device—Android, iPhone, Alexa, and even in the car dashboard through Android Auto and Apple CarPlay—this game changer enables the "anywhere, anytime workforce" concept to evolve as futurists have predicted. This is how to make work smart!

Targa is a leadership game changer. No other performance SaaS solution on the market today even comes close. It redefines how the organization connects the dots between goal setting and execution, automating much of the business process along the way to deliver hyper-performance.

To quote one of my Gartner analysts: "Targa is in a class of its own. It addresses a global problem that executives face every day when attempting to manage organizational performance. And unlike anything I've seen, Targa requires technologies from several Magic

Quadrants (Gartner classifies all technologies into quadrants to determine how competitors fair against one another) to create and operate the platform."

This statement says it all. Targa addresses a global problem that affects companies in every industry and of every size. As the wave of resistance continues to grow, poor performance is on the rise, and Targa is purposely built to reverse this trend.

How's this for a head-turner? Over 40 percent of goals in *Fortune 500* companies never come to fruition. This statistic is not guesswork but a fact that is reiterated time and again by management experts. This is an incredible number. Most of the blame can be pinned on action items that support goals getting lost in the weeds of execution, only to never get executed.

That is why Targa is so welcomed. It intrinsically collapses the gap between planning and execution. Relying heavily on automation to help get the job done, it dramatically increases the odds that goals will not get bogged down in execution, as it eliminates the disconnects, bottlenecks, and voids found in traditional approaches to produce results.

Automating work is a significant part of the solution. Leaders are often not aware of the many ways that automation can free up human hands and improve the ROI on human capital. Once on Targa, leaders become cognizant of the impact that performing mundane, routine work has on productivity. And without improving the productivity of teams, maximizing performance is impossible.

Case in Point: Senior Vice President—Major Retail Bank

With twenty-five vice presidents reporting to him, this senior VP (SVP) of a top-ten retail bank was responsible for generating a weekly summary report from every VP. The report was put together manually by each VP every Friday, and it took between 1 and 1.5 hours to complete the report. This was considered low-value work by the SVP and his VPs.

This is an example of repetitive, mundane work if there ever was one. The solution: a Targa action robot custom-built on the platform to automatically generate the report for each VP. This eliminated the need for the VPs to do anything but review the report once generated.

When asked what work the SVP would have the VPs do in lieu of preparing the reports, he immediately responded: customer acquisition. He turned this example into a revenue opportunity (52 weeks x 1.5 hours = 78 hours per VP saved, or 4,056 in aggregate among the 25 VPs.) He guesstimated the average hours VPs spent with clients to acquire new customers, determining that it could add 75 to 100 new customers per year to the region.

This senior leader became aware of the many ways that custom action robots on Targa can take over low-value work. Once the platform is in use, be it for a team, department, division, or an entire enterprise, the opportunities to automate work become obvious. Capitalizing on automation to optimize the collaborative process is a sign of good leadership.

Below is a more complex example of how bot-to-bot collaboration works on the platform in a sales situation. Note the sequential handoff between robots in a six-step process. Each action robot plays a specific role in getting work done. The chain starts with the predictive analytics robot and ends with the sales action robot. The aim of Targa is to make work smart, and this requires automating as much of the business process as possible.

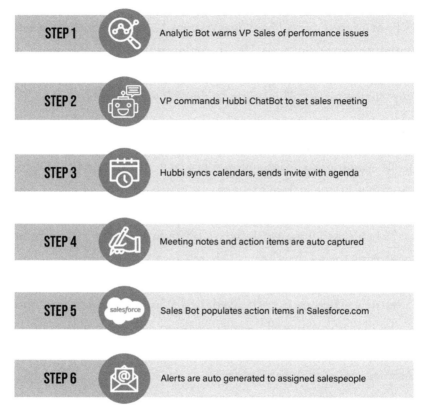

In this case, the sales VP was alerted to the situation by the predictive analytic robot running in the background that performance problems lie ahead. Once alerted, the VP used Hubbi, the command chatbot, to check calendars, schedule the meeting, and share the agenda. The meeting robot on the platform took over from there, automatically running the meeting, capturing team notes, and assigning action items. The platform's sales robot extracted the action items from the meeting and populated the information in Salesforce. com for salespeople to work on.

This is the power of bot-to-bot automation. Think of the number of meetings that you run every year. Now think of the productivity gains that could be garnered for you and your teams using Targa. Our experience demonstrates that gains of up to 50 percent productivity can be realized in a short period of time. Improve the productivity of team members and, by extension, improve organizational performance. It's that simple.

Early on in the book, we compared the collaboration age to the industrial age. During the first revolution, machines stepped in to perform low-value work. Take the automotive industry. Machines replaced human hands to make car parts, and humans performed more value-rich work like inspecting cars.

Replacing human hands was the intent then and is the intent today. In this revolution, instead of machines replacing human hands, technology is doing the job. Progressive leaders see Targa as the ultimate collaboration weapon to get the job done and attain hyper-collaboration!

Robots working in tandem to automate as much of the business process as possible is the way of the future. The trend to use robots wherever possible to perform low-value work will continue its stupendous growth. On the horizon, we see another phase in the automation journey barreling down on us—bot-to-bot decision-making.

Even Targa is not there yet, but it is on our strategic road map. This phase of the journey will spawn technologies that augment human intelligence. This will help leaders manage complexity in decision-making and reporting. In the on-the-fly world, humans alone are no longer capable of dealing with the complexity in decision-making. They need digital coworkers to help get the job done.

Certainly, these are extraordinary times! Around the globe, companies are jockeying for positions to compete on the battlefield of tomorrow. Adopting Targa to optimize the collaborative process moves the organization closer toward excellence. This is how leaders cash in on the AI gold rush. This is how you make work smart!

The Performance Quandary

This book repeatedly emphasizes that optimizing the collaborative process is the first step to maximizing performance and moving the organization closer toward excellence. This perspective greatly influenced how our team went about the process of identifying the invisible forces that drive excellence.

Consultants, coaches, and institutions teach the principles of excellence to help organizations achieve this pinnacle of success. That's what they do. They get leaders to concentrate on the things that matter in striving for excellence. For the most part, they view excellence as a destination. Below is an example of a list of hints put forth by a leading program on excellence.

KEYS TO WORKPLACE EXCELLENCE

1. Provide a compelling, positive vision with clear goals.

2. Communicate the right stuff at the right time.

3. Select the right people for the right job.

4. Create a united team atmosphere.

5. Encourage cool stuff—continuous improvement and innovation.

6. Recognize and reward excellent performance.

7. Demand accountability.

Training leaders how to achieve excellence through these types of programs is all good and necessary. However, following the sage advice of Tom Peters, we view excellence as a never-ending pursuit. This put us on a different track. We are not interested in understanding the principles of achieving excellence but understanding the underlying dynamics that move the organization toward excellence.

The forces we sought had nothing to do with the typical markers used by traditional KPIs or OKRs. These tools are, for the most part, trailing indicators of how the organization has performed but say nothing about the leading indicators to predict how the organization will perform. They are akin to a report card with grades. Our interest was to identify the forces that create good grades in the first place.

Achieving or moving toward excellence is a challenge. In silo-managed companies, it can be downright difficult. This industrial age approach to managing operations, albeit commonplace, is archaic. This is a major factor that stands in the way of improving performance, especially in large organizations. Moreover, it is not in keeping with the rules for good leadership in the modern era.

With the paradigm shift, structures that wall off functions are being replaced by more open, borderless structures. In essence, silo structures are performance killers. They tend to reward the wrong behavior and are not conducive to moving the organization toward excellence.

A colleague of mine, Dr. Dean Spitzer, is a highly acclaimed authority on performance measurement, author of several books on the topic, and a former performance thought leader at IBM. He has spent decades studying the subject and consulting to leadership teams in *Fortune* 100 companies.

Over the years, he espoused the notion that traditional reward systems are counterproductive to modern organization life, as they force leaders to focus on the wrong performance indicators. He further claims, "The quandary we face is that the performance of a silo or functional area of an organization becomes the carrot that executives chase."

He insists that silo structures are not conducive to measuring the right things regarding performance. Organizations that operate in functional silos possess measurement and reward systems that reinforce the silo mentality. He says, "This industrial age view of organizational life stands in the way of moving the organizations forward." Below is a graphic he uses to represent the silo-structured organization.

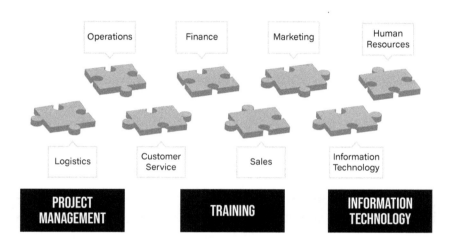

Spitzer believes organizations that manage operations through this kind of structure place themselves behind the performance eight ball. He contends, "Executives must move away from the silo-managed structures. It no longer has a place in modern business, as it forces the wrong behavior. The focus should be on measuring performance outcomes seen as value to customers and stakeholders, not as outputs of individual functions."

He demonstrates his logic using the illustration below. It emphasizes that silo organizations are geared toward measuring the outputs (what we produce) in a function versus outcomes (what value we create) for customers and shareholders.

He also believes that "anything in an organization that doesn't contribute value to outcomes should be considered cost and waste." And he presents a bulletproof case that many executives are being rewarded based on costs and waste, which flies in the face of achieving excellence, the ultimate prize.

For years, our firm has counseled leaders that reward systems based on silo performance will more than likely cost another silo dearly. When one silo does extremely well, it is often at the expense of other silos. This does not necessarily occur on purpose but as a natural extension of leaders keeping their eye on the prize—silo performance.

Getting the organization to move away from silo structures and toward open-border structures is not easy. When they are steeped in reward systems that pay off for the wrong reasons, trying to get large legacy organizations to move toward open structures is a bit like turning around the *Queen Mary* going full steam ahead: takes too long to stop, too long to turn, and then too long to restart. But try we must, and try we will.

Although we have seen dramatic progress in this area over the last decade, we still have a long way to go. My years have taught me that turning the *Queen Mary* is possible. The need to reward organizational performance seen as value delivered to customers and shareholders in the age of collaboration should be self-evident. This is another sign of good leadership.

Forces of Excellence

Excellence is elusive. It is meant to be chased and not caught. However, as the organization moves toward excellence, we assumed that there are intangible forces at work to help get the job done. It was these invisible forces that captivated our research.

Known as the Three Forces of Excellence, they are the leading indicators that the organization is moving toward excellence. Below are the forces with a brief description of each.

1. **Speed to Action**: This is the first critical force. In an age of collaboration where instantaneous equates to competitiveness, the speed with which information is converted into actionable solutions is what distinguishes an agile organization from a traditional organization. This force relates to the Information-to-Action Life Cycle discussed in chapter one. Focus on improving this force to move the organization closer toward excellence.

Case in Point: Managing Partner— Technology Consulting Firm

The owner of this technology consulting firm was working with the research division of a large high-profile hospital. Asked by the hospital leaders to use Targa to manage his initiatives and to report his progress to the executive director of the division, he quickly realized that managing his action items, which typically took forty-five minutes to one hour per day, was now taking eight to ten minutes per day.

Converting time saved into dollars, he estimated that by using the platform, his firm could bill an additional $12,000 to $15,000 in additional revenue per consultant annually. By improving the speed to action, this firm saw the opportunity to increase billable hours.

At the same time, the executive director believed that the consultant's weekly reports generated by Targa came in a form that he could easily understand and use to make decisions. He further admitted that communication between him and the consultant was made so much easier.

Since the platform auto-syncs the business process, the consultant generated a weekly report with a click of a button that instantly reflected the status of all initiatives and the action items that support them in one view. Reports archived on the platform provided the executive director a complete picture of what was planned and executed, providing him with all the information he needed to perform review sessions.

2. **Accuracy in Process**: This is the second critical force. Without a repeatable and scalable mechanism to manage the business process, there is no way to accurately tell where teams stand to reach goals at any given time. Recall the picture of how two leaders managed their meeting notes: one leader placed the notes in manilla folders and stacked them around the office while the other leader converted meeting notes onto Post-it Notes and tacked them onto a whiteboard to track progress. This is not an accurate way to participate in the collaborative process. Focus on improving this force to move the organization closer toward excellence.

Case in Point: Performance Manager—Healthcare Company

This leader was an expert in lean thinking (lean thinking is a term used to describe the process of making business decisions in a lean way). In his view, one of the greatest obstacles to improving organizational performance is the inaccuracy with which information is shared between workers. "This results in Muda," he scoffed.

"Muda," in the lean discipline, means wastefulness, uselessness, and futility. He went on to explain that accuracy in managing operations and making sound business decisions depends on the quality of information that is created and shared among team members from goal setting through execution.

Citing the problem, this leader found Targa to be the most efficient way to manage operations in a lean way. After several months of applying the platform, he recognized that the amount of waste in terms of time and resources spent on nonvalue tasks he considers Muda.

He estimates that Targa, on average, has reduced the redoes and follow-ups by 25 percent. He further commented, "Muda is normally viewed as tangible waste. However, there is more and more evidence that intangible waste, such as the accuracy of information, improves the productivity of workers—the first step in improving organizational performance."

3. **Accountability in Execution:** Accountability is the third critical force. It has been a bone of contention with leaders since work was organized. We highlighted the accountability issue in the Google study. It concluded that accountability is a responsibility of workers and the right of leaders to insist upon. This is where the command card often needs to be

played. If workers are not held accountable, then all efforts to make the right organization and technology decisions matter little. Focus on improving this force to move the organization closer toward excellence.

Case in Point: President— Strategy Consulting Firm

According to this senior leader, holding people accountable requires far too much of his time. He claims that improving accountability is a constant challenge and that it is not entirely his people's fault.

He sees the glass as half full: "A percentage of people intentionally will want to hide, but that is only half the equation. The other half is the use of disconnected tools that act as a barrier to help people collaborate." The heart of most team members is in the right place; they just have a difficult time communicating their status relative to achieving goals in a timely manner.

> If workers are not held accountable, then all efforts to make the right organization and technology decisions matter little.

"Targa is a godsend to improve accountability," he proclaimed. With teams collaborating on a single platform, he believes that the ability to know where teams stand to goal anywhere and anytime without getting them involved has produced a tenfold return on his time to better manage operations—to focus on the things that matter.

Let's put our last stake in the ground. Improving the productivity of workers is the most effective way to improve organizational performance. This is how leaders move the organization closer toward excellence. To be highly successful at this requires that the three forces work in harmony: speed to action, accuracy in process, and accountability in execution.

As you can see from the three simple examples presented above, these forces are measurable. They play an important role and need to be tracked. Targa automatically tracks them so leaders can determine the degree to which the platform improves the productivity of team members.

Time and again we have proved this to be the case. Focusing on these forces is another sign of good leadership. And to those skeptics who believe it is too simple—think again!

Summary

Targa is a first-generation SaaS performance platform that enables organizations to hyper-collaborate. The difference between collaboration using the fragmented tools of today and hyper-collaboration using a single platform that leverages the hybrid workforce concept is anything but trivial.

The paradigm shift occurring in organization life is not only changing how we design, conduct, and execute work; it is changing the tools needed to out-collaborate competitors. Awareness of the intangible forces that move the organization closer toward excellence is an essential part of remaining competitive.

Know that the three forces working together behind the screen foretell how traditional KPIs or OKRs will fare. To ignore these forces would be tantamount to committing performance suicide. The adage "the devil is in the details" is no more important than when attempting to move the organization forward—and details include the speed, accuracy, and accountability leaders bring to the process of producing results.

FOCUS FACTOR #5

To *outfocus* competitors, leaders must go the extra mile and adopt a first-generation AI-driven platform purposely built to help the organization hyper-collaborate.

- Leaders must focus on integrating workflow resources on a single platform that auto-syncs the business system to optimize the collaborative process.

- Leaders must focus on automating as much low-value work in managing the business process as possible to maximize the ROI on human capital.

- Leaders must focus on how managing business performance hands-free will keep them at the forefront of the anywhere, anytime workforce movement.

COMPETITIVE
ADVANTAGE

LISTEN TO THE EXPERTS

What and Why of Focus

As the transition between ages unfolds, the expectations on leaders continue to rise. Good leadership demands that leaders contend with the convergence of technology and the human element. Great leaders will want to know *what* performance experts and senior operating leaders think about the convergence and *why* obstacles that get in the way can be the death knell for competing on the battlefield of tomorrow.

THROUGHOUT THE BOOK, I have spoken to you as leaders in the generic sense. Now I speak to you as an individual leader.

It's your team, your department, your division, or your enterprise that is charged with driving business results. It's your responsibility to maximize performance and move the organization closer toward excellence, and it all starts with optimizing the collaborative process. And it's you who must decide if Targa is the right solution to keep your team at the forefront of the collaborative movement.

As the collaboration race rages on, competitors are feverishly vying for position. Below is the Focus Factor Road Map to help you get to the winner's circle. Know it well. Refer to it often as you prepare to contend with the convergence challenge.

Focus Factor #1

To *outfocus* competitors, leaders must overcome the fallout that on-the-fly leadership has on the Core Leadership Functions in building the collaborative organization of tomorrow.

Focus Factor #2

To *outfocus* competitors, leaders must hone attention skills to counter the blowback effect that leading on-the-fly has on their ability to volitionally focus on the things that matter.

Focus Factor #3

To *outfocus* competitors, leaders must be moving the organization forward, creating structures and work systems that quickly react to fluid market and competitive conditions.

Focus Factor #4

To *outfocus* competitors, leaders must be leveraging advanced technology to expand the capacity and capability of humans to perform work and optimize the ROI on human capital.

Focus Factor #5

To *outfocus* competitors, leaders must go the extra mile and adopt a first-generation AI-driven platform purpose built to help the organization hyper-collaborate.

Now ask yourself these questions:

- How will I contend with the fallout on my Core Leadership Functions: meeting management, decision-making, and reporting while leading on-the-fly?

- How will I contend with the blowback effect that Attention Deficit Syndrome has on my cognitive ability to volitionally focus on the things that matter while leading on-the-fly?

- How will I contend with leveraging people, structure, and work systems as I lean forward to move the organization closer toward excellence while leading on-the-fly?

- How will I contend with embracing the future of advanced technology to remain at the forefront of the race to out-collaborate competitors while leading on-the-fly?

- How will I contend with the opportunity to go the extra mile and enable the organization to hyper-collaborate while leading on-the-fly?

My job is done! I have answered the question that Clayton Christensen, our go-to innovation expert, would ask—what is the job to be done? For this book, it is getting you to "think again" about how you connect the dots between collaboration and performance to move the organization closer toward excellence.

If you are having second thoughts about the continued use of managing the business with fragmented resources at the ground level, then this book has done its job. Moving your organization onto a single AI-driven platform to manage the business is how you make work smart.

Now let's listen to what performance experts and senior operating leaders have to say about the challenge of contending with the convergence of technology and the human element and why now is the time to capitalize on the AI gold rush.

Listen to Experts

As a professor, author, consultant, senior researcher, and performance measurement thought leader at IBM, I have long been trying to convince executives that technology, no matter how sophisticated, is still just a set of tools that needs to be used intelligently and collaboratively to be effective. Most of what we call "business intelligence" and "artificial intelligence" must still be built on and reflect the need for humans to be more productive in contributing to results. In my book, *Transforming Performance Measurement*, I explain that organizations must measure the right things to be effective, referring to this process as "socialization of measurement." I explain that socializing measurement, especially as it relates to organizational performance, should follow the lead of human intelligence in a collaborative manner. I have seen tens of millions of dollars invested in technology tools while almost nothing is invested in helping people to effectively use them. In my book, I ask, "Is technology making measurement better or just more automated?" Clearly, we need better tools to manage operations, but we need to do this in a social context. Organizations are social entities. The best organizations are not the ones with the most powerful tools alone, but the ones that have the most effectively collaborative cultures and systems in which to harness the power of technology. I refer to this state of collaboration as interactivity, where conversations, experiences, and learnings turn data and information into knowledge and wisdom. Bill is right: it is only through collaboration driven by the convergence of technology and the human element that organizational life can be transformed and prepared to compete in a hyper-collaborative world. I am amazed that, despite the great advances in technology, our organizational systems are still quite primitive, which is further evidence that technology alone is not the answer. We need collaborative systems to enable the convergence of people and technology to produce the synthesis we call progress so the vexing problems surrounding collaboration that we face today can be solved.

—*Dr. Dean R. Spitzer*
Performance Management Innovator

Investing in and serving on the boards of several technology companies and now heading a NASDAQ healthcare technology company, I am fully aware of the importance of executives to get the convergence of technology and the human element right. This is especially true in my specialty of healthcare, where the race to leverage technology in patient care and company operations has risen to a fervorous pitch. Collaboration is not only an important subject; it is perhaps the most important subject of this century. Organizations who get this right will attract investors, talent, and customers, all of which are necessary to compete long term. We are at the early stage of a technology revolution the likes of which has never been experienced. Be proactive and not reactive and listen to Bill's plea, or risk the competitive consequences.

—Dr. David Milch
Chairman/CEO, Healthcare Capital Corp.

As a seasoned operating executive and management consultant, I marvel at the proliferation of collaboration tools and knee-jerk reactions by companies that continually seek to implement the latest instant communication, file sharing, and alert systems. This often creates confusion and sensory overload in the work environment since none of these so-called collaboration tools promote the necessary accountability or timely decision-making to stay aligned from goal setting through execution. Planning, especially strategic planning, is a critical function of leadership. However, the current array of tools available to plan and execute are woefully inadequate. Bill's approach completely changes our understanding of the connection between collaboration and performance and planning and execution. His assertion that the challenge of the century is contending with the convergence of technology and humans is well founded and relevant. This challenge looms large!

—Dan Taylor
President, Guidacent Consulting

Having worked with both computers and people my entire career, I can emphatically say, without reservation, that computers will never "outthink" humans. Organizations are only able to unlock value from information when they figure out how to optimally bring humans and technology-driven insights together in their decision processes. Deep learning algorithms can certainly "learn" the rules of a game through trial and error by mostly failing billions of times. Conversely, the human brain is miraculous in its ability to connect disparate pieces of information and fill in missing information that is not possible by any machine learning algorithm. The paradox is that humans must also be willing to allow new insights to inform their intuition, and that is where the convergence of technology and the human element comes in, and as Bill indicates, there is no better time in history to take advantage of the convergence like the present.

—*Gerhard Pilcher*
Founder/CEO, Elder Research

As president of a leading technology consulting firm, I provide advice to executives of *Fortune* 500 companies on how to strategically apply technology. I shrill when executives manage the business through silos. This practice stands in the way of creating an agile organization that promotes collaboration through technology across the enterprise. This is especially true in large legacy organizations. They are at risk to retain their market leadership position because of it. The chasm between strategic planning and execution is widening mostly caused by disconnected systems, pervasive use of paper-based processes, and continued use of humans to perform mundane tasks. The "future of work" evolution where organizations operate as intelligent enterprises is upon us. Leaders must understand the gravity of not properly addressing the convergence of technology and the human element now before it's too late. The clock is ticking. The gap between planning and execution can only be closed through AI-enabled automation. Without a better technology-based solution that seamlessly manages operations, shareholder and customer expectations cannot be easily met.

—*Vik Kasturi*
Founder/President, Digitivity

Having served many executive positions in finance, supply chain management, and data operations and as a consultant with PwC, I can attest to the many ways is which technology and humans will need to work side by side going forward. Especially in the post-COVID world, humans alone are no longer capable of managing all aspects of work. The workplace has become so complex and unwieldy that unless executives take full advantage of the gains that can be made in productivity by off-loading repeatable mundane tasks onto robots, they will not be competitive. The convergence is not hyperbole—it's reality. Executives that take advantage of the convergence will inevitably outperform competitors.

> Especially in the post-COVID world, humans alone are no longer capable of managing all aspects of work.

—*Barbara Miller*
Former VP Global Sourcing and Data Management, AmerisourceBergen

As a performance and quality expert holding several senior operating positions, I strongly recommend that leaders take advantage and capitalize on the convergence of technology and the human element now. Leading in a post-COVID workplace where the work-at-home movement dominates the landscape is here to stay. Leaders who do not accept the fact that this is the "future of work" are missing the boat. From a performance perspective, there will be no turning back, as the cost benefits to distance manage the business process have now been established. This is a do-or-die situation for many companies—so take Bill's proposition seriously!

—*Richard Chamberlain*
Manager Performance & Quality, Children's Hospital of Orange County

As a global executive with a career spanning many decades, I believe we are at a moment in time where technology is taking a functional leap forward. Due to the processing power available today, we can now enable new applications in AI that will change how we work and live forever. We are now just starting to see the beginning of the merge between technology and humans. The evolution of human-to-bot development is now being augmented by machine learning capability to achieve bot-to-bot decision-making. The leadership challenge is to not be afraid but to further support the convergence that is inevitable. Leaders must embrace the convergence with a vision for growth and possibilities. Not doing so can have grave consequences on the business. There is much as stake, so heeding Bill's words may do you well.

—*Juliette Samson*
CIO/Officer, VP Supply Chain World Finer Foods

As the owner of an executive search and human resource consulting firm for several years, the need for well-conceived strategic plans to optimize the ROI on human capital has never been greater. This applies from *Fortune* 100 companies to the SMBs where identifying, recruiting, and retaining the best talent has dramatically changed over the last decade—and is very costly. Leveraging collaboration to get a leg up on competitors is a critical dimension for consideration. In fact, when leading a consulting engagement, time and again I recognize how important it is for plans to include collaborative technology that sets a company apart and fits the present-day worker need for "balance." Without question, the convergence of technology and the human element is a significant aspect of talent-stacking the organization of tomorrow.

—Randy Samsel
Founder/CEO, eSearch Talent Solutions

For the last twenty-five years, I have owned a CPA firm that serves businesses in several industries and a coaching company that helps accounting firms across the globe become more profitable. If there is one thing that I have learned over my experiences, it's that performance is heavily dependent on how well organizations collaborate. When I refer to collaboration, I'm speaking about both sides of the proverbial ledger—how clients collaborate as a business and how accounting firms collaborate with their clients. I've never isolated the importance of collaboration on performance in the world of accounting until recently. Harnessing the power of collaboration is indeed a significant aspect to maximizing bottom-line performance, be it a company or an accounting practice. And the only way to get there is through advanced technology—that you can be sure of!

—Salim Omar
CEO, The Omar Group of Companies

For the past twenty-five years, I have been in the investment community serving as an investment banker, institutional investor, and private investor in early-stage firms. Companies looking to generate high ROICs (Return on Invested Capital) must be efficient with their resources, and there is no better way to accomplish this than by unifying workplace dynamics. This is increasingly true with a workforce that is more demographically diverse and geographically dispersed. From an investor perspective, the convergence of technology and humans is upon us, and for those leaders who take advantage of it, they will be able to streamline communication, automate work, and eliminate waste—the best of all worlds for stakeholders, shareholders, and customers.

—Shields Day
CEO, Daylight Capital Solutions

As an attorney and former business executive with past tenures at the NFL, NHL, and PGA Tour—and now in my own business law practice—I know all too well how important it is to effectively collaborate. To conduct business today requires companies to act and react in "hyperdrive" if they are to compete. On the horizon, I see many aspects of business that are about to take a 180-degree turn as advances in technology enable robots to perform mundane tasks while humans concentrate on more productive tasks. The convergence that Bill speaks of is here and will exact its toll on those who don't embrace the transformation. Be cognizant of it, recognize where you can take advantage of it, and, above all, ensure that you establish your position in the collaborative movement to *outfocus* competitors.

—Law Offices of Charlie Schmitt LLC.

ECLIPSE YOUR LIMITATIONS

Significant money and time are spent on joining the business process with technology in every industry. Answering the question "Where is it?" is not simple, and many companies have large staffs of data analysts and number crunchers to provide reports sometimes weeks and months after the fact. These stale, often out-of-date reports further confuse leaders as to where teams stand to goal when managing the business process at ground level.

This is workplace reality. Progressive leaders acknowledge the current state-of-affairs and possess the presence of mind and the temerity to do something about it. Ralph Waldo Emerson said, "The person you are destined to be is the person you decide to be." This statement is no more relevant than when applied to leadership.

Who you are as a leader and who you want to be as a leader are one and the same, according to Emerson. To eclipse your state as a leader requires asking the What and Why of Focus regarding leadership. Create a vision of who you want to be and address the obstacles that can get in the way of achieving that vision. This is a sign of good leadership.

Although there is overwhelming evidence that the tools and techniques used today are making the workplace an ever-more complex, almost unsustainable environment to get things done, most leaders will persist in staying the course. The Morse Curve predicts that only 15 percent of leaders will even consider using Targa to manage the business process at this stage in its life cycle. The reason: it's a disruptive solution that requires behavior change.

This book is intended to test your outer limits. Stretching your limitations is what distinguishes leading from managing. Great leaders know this and will adopt Targa to capitalize on the AI gold rush and change their organization's behavior forever.

Targa is by no means the first disruptive technology that requires behavior change. Here are a handful of other highly successful examples from the past:

> This book is intended to test your outer limits. Stretching your limitations is what distinguishes leading from managing.

- Long before Bill Gates introduced Windows, he watched an engineer at Harvard burn the midnight oil trying to get rid of the "green screen" on the opened desktop, prompting him to envision a menu displayed on the screen that changed behavior forever.

- Long before Steve Jobs and Steve Wozniak built the first Apple computer, they were building the blue boxes phone phreakers used to make free calls across the nation until they envisioned how a high-design desktop computer with a proprietary operating system would serve a niche market that changed behavior forever.

- Long before Sir Timothy John Berners-Lee invented the internet, he worked on the intranet until one day he envisioned how to make it accessible to everyone across the globe, changing behavior forever.

- Long before Mark Zuckerberg invented Facebook, two brothers at Harvard were hard at work figuring out a way to create a social platform for Harvard students to communicate while Mark envisioned communicating on a global scale that changed behavior forever.

The list goes on and on. These visionaries eclipsed the limitations accepted as the conventional wisdom for decades. Breakthroughs like these did not come without a price. These individuals withstood the ridicule that the naysayers served up, whispering in their ear that it would never work. These visionaries disregarded traditional thinking to bring new solutions to life that changed behavior forever, as is the case with Targa.

You stand at the crossroads, deciding whether to stay the course and continue struggling to keep pace or to eclipse your limitations and adopt Targa. As you make your decision, just realize that the future of work is upon us now, and standing in the way of progress can leave your organization vulnerable to becoming the next Sears, Eastman Kodak, or Motorola.

Managing the business process where humans, robots, and systems work in concert to produce business results on a single platform is now possible. This is a pivotal step in the evolution of the anywhere, anytime workforce movement. As advanced technology spreads its wings and flies into every corner of organizational life, it will continue to change how we design, conduct, and execute work.

Truly, business leadership today ain't what it used to be! As the race to harness the power of collaboration through automation takes center stage, no leader, great or otherwise, will willingly want to be left behind at the station. Follow the Five Focus Factor road map carefully and let Targa help your team hyper-collaborate to *outfocus* competitors and gain the competitive advantage.

Ten Leadership Bill-isms:

On-the-fly leadership—a modern-day phenomenon that produces fallout on how leaders perform the Core Leadership Functions.

Attention Deficit Syndrome—the inability of a leader to volitionally focus their attention on the things that matter, when they matter.

Cognitive Breakpoint—that point where the ability of a leader to lead completely shuts down and message processing, understanding, memory, and learning are not possible.

Convergence challenge—the tug-of-war between the pull of technology and the pull of human resistance to change.

Wave of resistance—the forces of workplace complexity and work overload that push against all efforts to move the organization forward.

The Six Ps—the asset categories (people, products, procedures, policies, property, and price) that customers use to determine the value of a product or service.

AI gold rush—a way to convey the current state in the evolution of technology as it relates to changing every facet of workplace and workforce dynamics.

Workplace singularity—a state in which leaders and teams think as one, act as one, and work as one in the process of producing results.

Change-ready culture—an environment where leaders and teams are well prepared to accept and embrace change as a fact of organizational life.

State-of-the-time—a term used to describe something new, innovative, and even revolutionary that is purposely built to address modern-day business challenges.

Useful Links

targatek.com

whitespacellc.com

CPSIA information can be obtained
at www.ICGtesting.com
Printed in the USA
BVHW040532260322
632228BV00002B/8/J